"*A great man is one who knows
that he was not put on earth
to be part of a process
through which a child can
be hurt.*"

—Murray Kempton

Today
Is for Children
Numbers Can Wait

HERB SNITZER

in collaboration with Doris Ransohoff

FOREWORD BY A. S. NEILL

THE MACMILLAN COMPANY · New York, New York

"*Being Alive,*" *from* The Complete Poems of D. H. Lawrence, *edited by Vivian de Sola Pinto and F. Warren Roberts, copyright* © *1964, 1971 by Angelo Ravagli and C. M. Weekley, is reprinted by permission of The Viking Press, Inc.*

Selections from The Me Nobody Knows: Children's Voices from the Ghetto, *edited by Stephen M. Joseph, copyright* © *1969 by Stephen M. Joseph, are reprinted by permission of Avon Books, New York.*

ALSO BY *Herb Snitzer*

Summerhill: A Loving World

The Macmillan Company
866 Third Avenue, New York, N.Y. 10022
Collier-Macmillan Canada Ltd., Toronto, Ontario

Library of Congress Catalog Card Number: 75-175595

FIRST PRINTING

Printed in the United States of America

To
KATE
with humility and love
this book is dedicated

Foreword

Summerhill has inspired quite a lot of schools. There is nothing wrong in inspiration; Summerhill itself was inspired by Homer Lane's Little Commonwealth. But there is a difference between inspiration and copying. If a school is set up simply in imitation of Summerhill, that is wrong—for that means a looking backward, a lack of originality, a lack of perspective. No school, Summerhill included, is the last word in education.

Herb Snitzer spent the best part of the fall of 1962 in Summerhill; he was a professional photographer then, and he was preparing his book, *Summerhill: A Loving World*. When he returned to America he began his own school at Lewis-Wadhams. Herb admits that Summerhill inspired him, but this new book shows that he is no slavish follower, no imitator, no disciple. We all go through a stage of discipleship, but if we do not come out of it we are inferior. A wise man does not label himself Montessorian, Steinerite, Deweyite, Summerhillian; to do so is to look backward.

Herb and his wife, Kate, have gone their own way, a way parallel to that of Summerhill. We share the same attitudes to children and freedom. We both have our community governments. We both try to abolish fear and adult authority of any kind. One great danger in school self-government is the personality of the school head. I have known schools with "self-government" where everything the headmaster proposed at a meeting was carried. Alas, half my proposals are outvoted. From the conversations with his pupils that Herb has recorded in this book, I feel that he tries to keep his own personality out of it as much as he can. The personality cult is a danger to any government, of school or country. Benevolent authority is more dangerous than strict authority, always; a kid can rebel against a stern teacher, but not against an amiable one.

The difficulty with descriptions of free schools is that often the reader is led to believe they are Paradises. I get many letters that speak of the Summerhill "Paradise," and I suppose that Lewis-Wadhams gets the same kind of overpraise. No one who has lived in Summerhill will call it a Paradise, and I am sure that Herb and Kate will strenuously deny that their place is an ideal home. Schools like ours get too many problems dumped on them to come within miles of Paradise. This book is an honest description; it does not try to make the Lewis-Wadhams geese into swans. Herb writes frankly about his failures—he hasn't yet reached the height of my cunning in claiming that Summerhill successes are due to the school and its failures to the home (although there's some truth in that).

It is very important, I think, that Herb quotes at such length what the children said to each other and to him; their conversations illustrate the school in a way more intimate— and more direct—than any teacher's description of freedom. The children who come to Lewis-Wadhams are inured to a world of pollution, class war, cheap criteria of values. The forces of reaction are infinitely more powerful than the forces of progress and humanitarianism, and our free schools are little islands in an ocean of anti-lifeness. A few people like Herb and Kate are trying to give some of these children from the sick environment a chance to live life fully and bravely and charitably, and their conversations reflect this.

Freedom for youth is in the air, and a book like this is timely and cogent, for too many think of youth's challenge as violence. Violence never cured anything. The violence of the Russian Revolution in 1917 led to freedom in schools, freedom about sex, but it ended in a police state with no individual freedom at all. No, the way of rebellion against paternalism is not violence; it is the slower way of practical work for freedom, and that is the message of this book—to let kids be themselves, and in a few generations the world will become healthy and happy.

There is no shortcut to this end, and to treat adults is not the way. The thousands of patients under therapy in the Western world are, in the main, not folks who will redeem society. As Reich used to say, "If you bend the tree as a twig, it will never be quite straight." The answer is not therapy; it is prophylaxis, abolishing the evils that make people neurotic and anti-life. This is what Lewis-Wadhams is doing. The tide of freedom for children is flowing—but we must be careful to prevent our work from being used in the wrong way. I am told that in the United States some of the new free schools are becoming political, thus canceling out the idea of freedom, which means no indoctrination of any kind. I see no symptoms in this book of Herb's doing so anti-freedom a thing. Discussions in the school are wide-ranging—racialism, sex, anything the children think of that is of interest to them—but no indoctrination, religious, political, whatever, which is the negation of freedom. Lewis-Wadhams means being a free individual in a free society, as opposed to being an unfree person in an unfree society.

The only hope for the world is the abolition of "character-molding," of that authority in home and school that gives children a slave mentality for life. A nation of molded children produced Hitler. History and geography are forgotten when one leaves school, but the emotional molding lives on. Reich said it thirty years ago; Godwin said it in 1785.

The function of Lewis-Wadhams, and of Summerhill and the new schools, is to fight the mass molding that makes the world an evil place. We pioneers think of education as living, not the exam system set by the Establishment that faces every child who wants to succeed in a profession or trade. Picasso could not get a job teaching art in a British or American school because he had not passed any exams.

At eighty-eight I cannot live to see the results of Herb's work; but I have no doubt that it will have an influence on other schools in America and outside its borders. I hope that this book will have a large public, and I think that it will.

A. S. NEILL

ACKNOWLEDGMENTS

Many thanks are in order here. To the fifty-four children and sixteen other adults who share the joy and heartaches of Lewis-Wadhams; to the memory of W. E. B. Du Bois and Robert Kennedy; to Mary Tur for her patience in typing this manuscript; to Doris Ransohoff, my friend and collaborator, for her insights, intelligence and endurance during those endless hours of working, watching and seeing a book being born; and lastly to my wife and equal partner in Lewis-Wadhams, Kate, for being who she is.

He who destroys one human soul is regarded as though he has destroyed a whole world; while he who preserves one soul within humanity is regarded as though he had preserved the whole world.

Mishnah Sanhedrin
THE TALMUD

Introduction

A book can do violence to what is basically a continuous living experience. Yet because I feel I have something to say, to express about the world of Lewis-Wadhams I live in, a book is born, limitations and all.

I used to be a professional photographer-journalist. It had its satisfactions. When you click the shutter of a camera at a given moment, you know that what you are recording in that split second is a moment of life lived. You know that the reality of that moment will always be there. The people will always be alive, the happening—incident or situation—will always retain its sense of the present. There it is for others to feel and to know as the photographer felt and knew it.

I hope that some of this sense of the present, of time lived —experienced in day-to-day terms, in terms of changing seasons and altered landscapes and of persons and places and feelings, of unaccountable mood swings and rhythm changes— is in this book. It is not meant to answer all questions about life in a "free" school, or to add more data to the already mountainous accumulation of information a materialistic world gathers in seeking to program its how-to-rear-children machine. It is not a survey or even an overall view of Lewis-Wadhams. It is my view, my experience of some of the things that happen when children and adults try to live as openly and directly with one another as they can.

I am only one person among many who contribute to the Lewis-Wadhams world. There is the underpaid and over-worked staff. There is my wife Kate. And there are the people who are our good neighbors in the small North Country townships which surround us. The Town of Lewis, population 750, is home most of the time to the fifty-four children and some of the seventeen staff members, all of the time to me and my family and to those of our staff who have always lived here and who have been the heart and loyal core of Lewis-Wadhams practically since the beginning, eight years ago: Barbara and Clyde Lambert, Vina and Jane Marble, and Margaret Phinney.

The grass is green in Essex County, the streams are full, the air is clear and the skies vast above the peaks and ridge-lines of the Adirondacks, but wallets are slim and job opportunities scarce. It is one of those upstate rural communities city people speed past on the Northway, sometimes vacation in to get back to the earth and are wont to call picturesque. It is not picturesque. It is beautiful and it is poor.

City-bred and a "liberal-radical" Democrat, I found the patience and stoicism of my country neighbors, their fatalism in the face of seemingly overwhelming odds, incomprehensible when I first came here. I have no doubt they found me equally difficult to understand and my intransigence a waste of time and effort. Over the years we have learned from each other and work together on local issues, on county boards and community fund-raising drives, with a growing acceptance on both sides.

Many of the children who were part of this year recorded, 1968–69, are no longer with us. Some have gone on to college, others are working, some have been taken out by parents or have left of their own accord. Their places have been taken by others, and tomorrow there will be still other children, presently unknown to us.

How Lewis-Wadhams will be in the future years or in what direction the community will go is difficult to say, as it becomes increasingly difficult to say what is going to happen to American society as we know it now or in what direction we as a nation and as a world will move.

In an increasingly technocratic, techtalitarian and monolithic society, the desire for life diminishes. With the knowledge that man now has the power to destroy himself and all life around him, faith in the value of one's own life and in the ability of one's own life-force to sustain itself withers away. The desire for life, at least in some of us, grows stronger in the face of such terrible odds.

The desire to live is personal, its presence—or absence— expressed in ways both solitary and social. When this desire no longer exists, man will die, with or without the megaton bomb. The history of world civilizations has shown that most nations die of internal atrophy.

I think you can see the evolutionary processes of nations in the evolutionary history of one child. One child is a microcosm of the world's attitudes, wishes and desires to sustain life or to obliterate it. There is a drive to exist and to have an identity, to search out what is basically pleasurable and fulfilling. There is also a drive to turn one's face to the wall, to deny feeling and to refuse freedom. Which way will it be?

Lewis-Wadhams is no panacea. We guarantee nothing. In some ways it is a miracle that we are still alive. In 1963 we stood almost alone in this country. Today there are many other schools offering children and adults the chance to live and let live within a framework of freedom and security. It is a good sign.

H. S.

Lewis, New York
February 18, 1971

AUTUMN

ENTRY I

The snows have come early to the North Country. We do not commonly feel the full thrust of winter until well into December. But three days ago, with Thanksgiving still a good two weeks off, we awoke to the white and still morning of our first snowfall. It has been snowing ever since, a soft, slow drift of white covering the far hills, the roofs of the school buildings, dorms and classrooms, which lie in random clusters in the broad valley below our hilltop house. The snow all but obliterates the shapes of the dark pines and elms, the paths and roads and fields and distant farmhouses.

Today the sun is out, the snow has stopped falling, and the air is crisp and cold. No vote is necessary, but a consensus clear among the seven- and eight-year-old members of my early morning math class: numbers can wait. We go sledding on the back hill.

I agree. Numbers can wait. Time is on the side of little children. Tomorrow is for numbers, today for the first snowfall of the year. Firsts are firsts, after all, occur but once and ought not to go uncelebrated. They are part of the "do you remember?" game to come. They are also part of the present, urgent, meant-to-be-lived now.

This present is also experienced today with by no means the least sense of immediacy by our youngest, Sigrid. She is sixteen months old, her world filled from moment to moment with wonder, joy, awe, as she happens upon things never before known to her. Her eyes are open and bright, and today questioning, as she confronts the strange new look of a familiar landscape.

She touches, smells and tastes the snow. She falls down in it, she eats it, she has a sled ride. She gets tired and wet and hungry. She is taken home to a warm bath, her bottle, her blanket, a lap and a rocking chair, her mother's voice. She falls asleep.

The main house smells steamy, of wet wool and beef stew, and is more boisterous than usual at lunch time.

ENTRY II

Craig is sixteen. He is a slightly built, fragile-looking boy, whose deepset dark and restless eyes belie the ease of his body's movements. He finds it hard to look at the one he is talking to—in this case, myself. He has come this morning to show me something he has written and that he wants to talk about.

It is Friday. Friday always turns out to be a day of many conferences and meetings. More than most. I don't quite know why. It begins like any other day—my math class, then midmorning in my office in the staff house where Craig comes to find me.

We settle down in the parlor to talk. Craig sits cross-legged on the old wicker settee. The staff house is a pleasant, old-fashioned farmhouse, my office, under the eaves of a re-modeled sun porch, narrow, but a new unbroken sweep of desk lends a spare modern grace to the serenity of the old. With its peaceful view of the valley, of now snowy fields and mountains beyond, my office suits me. It is a good place to work in. The parlor is warmer and it is cozy. The scarred old library table, heirloom of a former owner, is strewn as usual with an assortment of papers and journals, books, staff mail, read and unread, a bowl of homegrown, slightly crabby apples. The floor is littered with packages opened and un-opened, wet boots, and a cluster of empty milk bottles by the back porch door. A pot of Sanka on the stove.

Craig, I sense, tranquil though he looks, would rather pace than sit in contemplation of his thoughts or of my face as I read what he has written. I suggest Sanka for both and read:

In X school four years ago I met Bud. We opposed authority together and escaped into other worlds. . . .

X is a military-type all-boys prep school, the sort some par-ents, frequently fathers, are prone to think will straighten their boys out.

Craig again:

My impression of the real world, what I call the straight world, is ugly, living a lie, not being honest with yourself—that is, myself—conceited, mean, short hair, college and dress-up and being uptight, holding in my feelings like I think my parents want me to. So when I have to go back and live in the straight world I'll wear my hair long and look sloppy and look down on the straight people so I wouldn't feel a part of them. . . .

Craig had short hair when he arrived here two years ago. Today he wears his hair like a bush. He wears corduroys and over them an old flannel shirt several sizes too large, a string of beads which he has made. He goes barefoot.

> Craig:
>
> Here, the fantasy world I had with Bud doesn't work any-more. Maybe I will have to let go of him to grow. From you and the staff here I get a good feeling even though you don't escape [from] reality. But I don't know which to believe. This good real world or inhibited real world I think I will be in if I go to college or do anything to make me feel part of the straight world. . . .

This is not the language Craig's parents use to describe the ambitions they have for their son, the world in which they want him to assume his proper and privileged place. They do not see themselves the way Craig sees them. Sometimes I think they do not see their son at all—apart, that is, from his failure to meet their standards.

> Craig:
>
> Anyway, I put myself down for being scared of college. Maybe like you said, I don't want to face it, even though it would be a good place to learn. I'm scared by what I want to learn. I'm scared to get involved in learning and committing myself. . . .

Craig was a brain when he first came here two years ago. He still is, but he is other things as well. His talents are pro-tean. He has tried them all: poetry, music, art, acting, film-making and, not the least of all gifts, friendships. Quick to sense the feelings of others, he has learned to be increasingly articulate about his own. He is not afraid to smile when he is happy, which is more often than it used to be.

For the record, it is worth adding, I think, that Craig does not come from what people like to call a "broken home." He is not an only child. His family is neither poor nor black, "culturally disadvantaged" nor without prestige in the affluent middle-class society to which they belong. A society in which Craig feels destiny, in the form of his father, has fingered him also for the role of a "wheel."

Craig:

When I think of my father in relationship to college, my reaction is escape. I might feel the old pressures. . . . Don't do anything at all, because it's like my bad experience at X. I'm afraid I'll lose myself if I go into the straight world.

Craig is a real boy, although his name is not Craig. His fears are real fears. His feelings about the "straight world," peopled with authority figures who will try him constantly and constantly find him wanting, are the feelings of many here and elsewhere.

Craig and I talked for an hour or more. It is the prospect of the forthcoming Christmas holiday which has him uptight again. These three short weeks he will spend at home seem to encapsulate for Craig the whole of his besieged lifetime, the years that went before LW and those that will follow. It is a matter of his survival, a struggle—as he sees it—in either/or terms. A mythological struggle. To a large degree, a symbolic struggle.

Craig:

When I go home, or think of going home, the things that don't matter so much here become important there. For instance my hair, 'cause if I cut it I'll lose myself. . . .

He talks about my hair, the fact that I look clean and generally neat, that I polish my shoes, that I even put on a tie—his voice gets high here—when I go to Elizabethtown to the Office of Economic Opportunity meetings.

"*Do* I become another person when I put on a tie or wear a suit? Does this change me? Do I become someone else?"

"No, you don't, Herb. Or, at least," Craig smiled, "at least I don't *see* you as someone else."

The question is, Craig, how do you see yourself? Only I do not ask this. There is no need to. It is as plain to Craig as it is to me that who he is, what makes him uniquely Craig—the Craig of this moment dominated by fears and anxieties and needs, the Craig of tomorrow still a question mark—is a matter to be determined neither by one world's ways or another, neither by his father's notions of who he is nor by mine, but by his own.

He goes off, feeling better about himself, I think. After all, he has had success here, and he knows it. Success on his own terms, and he knows that too. Shifting, unsure, wavering though they may be, they are Craig's terms. No one has told him who he has to be. He has not been abandoned and will not now be deserted because he has shown himself to be still part child and frightened by old childhood shadows. He may fail again, he says, in the old ways, on the old terms, and so he is scared.

Is this really it, I wonder. Or is it the beginning knowledge of his own strength he is really scared of? This happens to a lot of children who have been hurt, somewhere along the line mutilated in their notions of themselves. One day they come up smiling, sort of happy. Sort of, because joy, a newly confident self, turn out to be not all that easy to live with. Dare one believe in it, I ask myself. Can one live up to it? And so I find myself wondering, not for the first time, which is the more threatening—fear of failure or fear of success, fear of fear or fear of joy.

It goes on for a lifetime, this continuously evolving process of learning about oneself, once committed to the idea of freedom. There is advance and retreat, now opening oneself up to the fullness of life, now taking cover, fearful once more of "losing oneself"—as Craig puts it—in that very fullness.

Entry III

Saturday morning's regular meeting was enlivened by something wonderfully funny and a little sad. The Saturday meeting is a fairly reliable index of the way things are going around here. A long meeting usually means we've got troubles. Something has gone wrong somewhere. The emotional climate suffers. Whatever it is, people then want to air their thoughts and feelings about it, often at length and stormily.

This term the community has settled into a good working, flowing rhythm. That means short meetings, like this morning's. I was glad, because I had hurt my back yesterday in a free-for-all snowball fight. (Funny, how staff as well as children seem to acquire unerring aim when the target is me. Why don't I learn to duck? Right on.) I was looking forward to the solace of a heating pad, a glass of wine and the various other comforts of a quiet Saturday afternoon at home before the fire.

Steve had something to say at the meeting, just before it broke. Steve is a fat boy. He is thirteen.

I pay a lot of attention to people's body attitudes, the kind of body energy a person gives off, how a person—child or adult—sits, stands, moves, hunches his shoulders, flexes his fingers, crosses his legs, smiles, frowns, slumps, sprawls. A host of small signals are communicated this way. One can sense, for example, almost at once an uptight presence or a fairly free and open one.

It is nothing new to relate tenseness of body attitudes (my unyielding back?) to tenseness of emotional attitudes. Rigidity of one sort is almost certain to betray itself in the rigidity of the other. On a more complex level, it is also possible to see in body attitudes the variety of physical disguises people assume to mask the way they feel about themselves.

These disguises—defenses, if you will—may be assumed with grace and sophistication. Craig is superficially at ease, moves with elegance and fluidity. Steve is another story. He is simply the classic "fat boy," a sad grotesque.

Fatherless, product of a series of indifferent foster homes and a succession of the usual abrasive public schools, Steve seems to sum up all the hidden hungers flesh—particularly fat flesh—is heir to. Without attempting any facile generalizations about the nature or dynamics of fatness, I find myself thinking of it—certainly in Steve's case—as a sort of sheath protecting its owner against the pain of his own anger, his sense of deprivation, and most of all, perhaps, his minimal feelings of self-worth.

Like other fat boys, Steve transmutes the self-contempt his fatness betrays into the bravura of the clown. He plays court jester. He looks upon himself as a figure of fun. Only the fun is not always funny. The humor has a cutting edge, rarely leaving his audience intact. As with most court jesters, his is a public image. His private encounters are meager, his friendships thin, but he is beginning to have them. These days I get the impression he is not quite so lonely, his jokes not so often at someone else's expense.

No one around here defines as virtue patience, forbearance or tolerance. No one defines virtue at all, which is not to say it does not exist. There is a lot of talk about and thought given to being oneself, fulfilling one's own wishes, finding one's own ways of ego and body satisfaction and not interfering with others. This leads to much noisy argument, meetings about who did what and to whom and had he a right to. On the other hand, it also seems to lead in the end to a live-and-let-live attitude, an I am I and Thou art Thou acceptance of other people's "things" or "hang-ups" or "bags." The result is an ambiance of extraordinary patience toward all but the most outrageously wounding behavior or the most relentless invasions of privacy.

I don't know what name to give this ambiance. Call it compassion, perhaps. It isn't always around, but when it is, it helps people, "new kids" like Steve especially, who are not used to it and need it the most, because as traditional authoritarian forms of control are relaxed, inner feelings begin to surface. How to handle them? (Long buried, they may be threatening.) Deny them? Share them? Weep over them? Laugh at them?

Steve asked for the floor:

I would like to propose that for the next two days a certain couple of persons present be asked to change their names. They're only visitors, I know, and won't be here long, but it's going to be awfully hard for me to spend even the weekend calling them Dick and Jane.

So much for the abrasions of the public school system! Dick and Jane, the visitors, became compliant, and laughing, offered the alternative of their family names. Motion made, seconded and passed. Meeting adjourned.

Monday, 18 November—
Thursday, 28 November (Thanksgiving)

Entry IV

A dismal, cold and overcast weekend followed by rain, rain, rain, and the beginnings of a melancholy November thaw. As usual, visitors over the weekend, in addition to Dick and Jane, parents, friends of staff. Weekends are when they all come—parents, prospective students, prospective teachers, staff relatives, friends of "experimental education" and just plain friends of somebody or other up here. The inevitable talk sessions, whether they take place down the hill in my office or up the hill in our living room, generally break down into a question-and-answer sort of pattern. Why we do what we do, why we don't do other things, whether children really learn (they do), whether we really practice democracy (we try to), whether we aren't afraid of "free" sex (we're not), how we feel about drugs (we're against them), where we get our teachers (good question), what our philosophy of education is, what school we belong to—are we structured or unstructured, progressive, permissive, Montessori-type, Neill-type, essentialists or perennialists—do we accept disturbed children, are we a kind of Utopia, do we recommend the Pill, are we pacifists, interracialists, monogamists, Marxists, atheists, agnostics or practicing Catholics, Jews, Baptists, Methodists, Quakers or Episcopalians.

I should make it plain that nothing much is ever rigid around here—worked out finally and forever. Education as an evolving process goes right on evolving for adults—staff and administrators—as well as for children, at least so far. It is not change for the sake of change I am talking about. It is rather that, as I am beginning to learn after six years of living the Lewis-Wadhams experience, any statement of policy, of theory, of dynamics, of structure, is reliable and valid only when it works. When and why it works depends, in turn, on a set of variables on a variety of levels.

Take a school full of "new kids," for instance. It has an entirely different feeling tone to it. So does a term full of new staff. Theoretically solved problems become unstuck again. Structure is subjected to merciless assault. The limits of democracy are tested to the utmost, as are the limits of personal freedom.

These periods and others like them can be unsettling, the less so the more clearly it is understood, really grasped, that the forms one has evolved only have viability if they are responsive to children's needs, rather than the other way around. Beyond the truth that humanness lies at the root of this business of education—of learning, growth, development, of child-rearing, or rather, people-rearing—I don't know that I have yet found any other so-called eternal verities. There is no other raft to cling to when the going gets rough. And it does.

If some of the forms we have evolved have gone under, some have survived, flexible, yet sturdy enough too to work under diverse conditions. One of these is team-teaching. Another is the seminar workshop for teen-agers. Both came about when we as administrators and teachers began to be free enough of preconceived notions to listen to what the children were telling us about what they needed.

We have had seminars over the last four years in history,

religion, reading and writing, sociology, sex, philosophy and government. There is nothing particularly new about the seminar as a learning-teaching form. We did not think it up certainly and were, in fact, slow to think about it as a possible solution to the teen-ager's need for total commitment, to be "saturated" with the subject matter that interested him. Classically, the seminar form evolved out of what was happening and what was not happening to the teen-agers locked into the traditional time slot of the hour class.

Either they did not come to class at all, came a few times and dropped out, or came for the sacred hour and stayed for three. It was after one of these marathon sessions that Kate, who was then teaching in the humanities, suggested that we forget about the hour class and give the teen-agers what they clearly were asking for. Viewed in the light of experience, the hour session began to look absurd. An anachronism, a hangover from a system generally conceded to be a failure from almost every point of view. We abandoned it.

It simply is not true that a thirteen-year-old cannot concentrate on one area of subject matter for more than an hour. To the contrary, if at all, then the more the better seems to be the case. And that is the way it has been ever since, two hours a day, five days a week, spent in one subject area for as long as student involvement can carry it.

The seminars are hard work for staff as well as students. They can be intense and intensely satisfying, and a whole lot of learning can happen on human as well as on academic levels. They can, on the other hand, be duds.

What is going wrong with "Do You Think White?" ?

Our first meeting (last week, Wednesday):

Mark: I'm walking down the street, my own street I mean, one time last summer. There aren't any black people living around there, not that I know of, anyway, in my neighborhood. So when I saw this Negro woman coming down the street, probably a cleaning woman, I just stopped and looked at her.

Herb: Something about what you just said strikes me as a little unusual. Don't you think so?

Mark: No, what? What did I say?

Herb: You said "probably a cleaning woman" about this black person you'd never seen before. Why did you say that? Mightn't she have been a doctor, or a lawyer, or a sociologist? Was she dressed in a particular way to suggest "cleaning lady" or what?

Mark: No, no particular way.

Herb: You just assumed she was a cleaning lady?

Dawn: That's not fair to Mark, Herb. He already said he lived in an all-white neighborhood. It's only natural to feel that way.

Herb: If it's only natural to feel that a black person you've never seen before in your neighborhood is a cleaning lady, then maybe we'd better have a look at what else you think is only natural for you to feel about black people.

Marti: Well, what if she was a cleaning lady. Is that necessarily a put-down?

Herb: Sure it is. Just to take it for granted she was. A lot of basic assumptions . . .

Maria (the only nonwhite present): Like the way they say "you people . . ."

Marti: Athletes and soul music, you mean, you're supposed to be good at.

James: Well, it's sort of true, though. Take, like, my mother. She thinks she's pretty good at dancing the twist. She's not near as good as a lot of blacks I've seen.

Herb: Here's another thing I want to bring up. About

Mark's cleaning lady. What difference would it make how she happened to earn her living?

Voice: Come on, man, that's really reaching!

Herb: Is it? Would you feel it necessary to tell us the same kind of thing about a white woman you had never seen in your neighborhood before? What you thought she did for a living?

As racism is more or less endemic to middle-class white America, why be surprised hearing our nonwhite children called "big-lipped," "baboon-faced" and so on? Name-calling is infantile. It expresses feelings of powerlessness. It is regressive. All children regress from time to time. But what is regression if not a return to basically unconscious attitudes, fears, wish-dreams, fantasies? And do not the roots of prejudice lie precisely in these unconscious or ill-remembered regions of early childhood? Let's get it out in the open, then, and look at it.

This was my reasoning, and I had brought the subject up at one of our Friday night discussion groups.

Anyone can come to the Friday night sessions. We hold them in the library, and although it is generally the older students who do most of the talking, middle kids and even little ones are often to be found lying on their bellies on the floor or curled up in somebody's lap listening. Anyone can start a subject going. Last Friday I did. I began to talk about racism.

Protestations of innocence, counterattacks and denials. No one meant anything by it, nothing racist, that is. All the same, we began talking about it and continued to do so for two nights running. When the second night's session was over, and a lot of stormy discussion still going on, I suggested we might get a seminar going to attempt to find out something about what this country really feels like to black men and women and to black children. Seven children decided to take a journey of "exploration" into the territory of black-experienced America. That is how "Do You Think White?" began.

Second meeting (Thursday):

James: What you were saying last time, Herb, was that there is such a thing as feeling "white."

Herb: Right, and that's where the in-built racism starts, right there.

Dawn: Then how can you ever feel what it's like to be black? I mean "feel black" if you really "feel white"?

Marti: Like that picture of Tommie Smith and Carlos in Mexico City. They're saying, "Up yours, man."

Mark: With black gloves on, "Up yours!"

Maria: You win the cup and you, like, still ride in the back of the bus.

A bibliography has been culled from our various personal bookshelves as well as from the school's library. Collections of essays, fiction, poetry, plays, history, songs, recordings, photographs, newspapers, magazines, *Ebony, Ramparts, Freedomways Quarterly*, the *Amsterdam News*. People take on assignments to read and report back. We begin by reading aloud James Baldwin's letter to his nephew: *The Fire Next Time.*

Marti: Wow, how would you answer that one?
Herb: Well, how would you?

Marti wrote:

The way James Baldwin described the love between his family was very beautiful. You know, the part about the father as a

little boy falling down the stairs, and James or his Grand-
mother picking him up and wiping away his tears. It made me
feel like I know his family and so often Negro or Black means
an issue, and not a people real and human, loving and crying.
It's probably a hangover from the time of slavery to now, that
blacks are slaves and slaves are not people.

Discussion: The plight of the black man used as object
serves the interests of an oppressive society. Objects are
manipulable. People stop being objects when they refuse to be
pushed around any longer. Not unlike put-down of children
by a culture basically harsh and insensitive to what they are
all about. Tentative and possibly threatening correlation
made. Feeling black, feeling nobody. Feeling powerless. Discussion lags. Retrieved by the lunch bell.

Next meeting: On Black Power.

ENTRY V

Letters appear on my desk from time to time, or are
handed to me. So are stories, poems and drawings. I answer.
A correspondence develops.

Today brought me this, from a thirteen-year-old:

Hurray for nice people.
I am all golden and mellow and light rain inside.
I am much too beautiful right now to read my beautiful story.

Another:

Herb,

I have to talk to you very soon before the end of term. I
have to talk to you about that letter I sent you (if you got it
yet!) and another thing too. Please talk to me.

Love,
Donna

Another:

Dear Herb,

Greetings friend. Sorry about that opening but I am very insecure. It is now about 8:20 P.M. It's very dark out and there is hardly any wind. I like it that way. Today I took a walk down to the brook. . . .

Herb, I just want you to know that I'm deathly afraid of you. Well, I guess I'm not deathly afraid of you but I'm pretty scared. . . .

I don't know, maybe I'm just too young to get along with you. I guess I just want to be around you without being scared. It's like so many people are talking to you all the time that I just think you won't hear me if I say anything. I guess I'll feel different sooner or later. It's getting late so I'll stop soon.

I just had a grapefruit for snack, I believe it was the most beautiful grapefruit I have ever had. Dave R. just made a beautiful cake. Banana nut bread I believe. I want some of

Remember that letter I sent you? The last one? Well I'm glad you understood what I was trying to say. . . . Please answer this letter when you have time. . . . Good night!

> With lots of my love,
> Chloe P.
> alias Pucci

p/s: You don't have to or anything, but sometime later on in the year maybe take a walk with me.

This one, a little book with crayon drawings:

Herb, I love you more than . . .

Flowers
and Rain Bows
And Rain
and snowflakes
And trees
and Magic!

Near term's end, correspondence multiplies.
From a staff member:

I have left. I would have told you all if I could have but it would have been too hard for me. I would have left anyway, since as you know it is very difficult for me to relate any more than superficially with anyone. It is that problem and the overwhelming feeling of emptiness that goes along with it that convinced me that leaving was the only solution. I realize you would have been willing to help but I couldn't ask for it . . . not from people I know. I guess if I need help I'll have to get it elsewhere. I think my leaving can't be detrimental to the community. If I'm fucked up on the inside, there's nothing to give or gain on the outside. . . .

Entry VI

Thursday. Again my morning math class of six- to ten-year-olds was displaced. Two meetings instead. The first was called by a twelve-year-old who wanted to leave his group, called the "Dome Kids" because they meet for classes in one of the school's new Bucky Fuller Domes. He wanted to join the "Little Room Kids." The second meeting was called by one of the latter.

The Little Room is in the barn, a rambling old red building across the road from the main house and dormitories, a split-level affair sloping down to the old stables where the sheep doze in winter, our bull calf rests, where the chicken coops are and the kids go to collect eggs, where there is a pond for ducks, the neglected remains of the orchard, our summer garden and the playing fields stretching away to meadowland and willows by the side of the brook. Besides the Little Room, the barn also houses a sewing room, our art room, pottery room and music room, wood-working shop, and on the lower level garages, bikes, tricycles, garbage truck and sundry other school vehicles.

The Little Room is a place apart. It is a kingdom of its own. It is really three rooms: two book- and picture-lined alcoves mainly for classes and one—the largest—for play, with blocks, ladders, easels, a piano, a zinc-lined table for water play, a cook stove for cookie baking, clay, swings, any number of rag dolls, bean bags and cubby holes. The Little Room is loved by many older children, and today was not the first time that an entry permit had been formally requested, or that official status—the right to membership in the younger group—had been sought. A warm and open, basically physically structured environment expressive of the sensual, tactile, and physical needs of young children, the Little Room, like childhood itself, belongs to little children. And, like childhood, one does not necessarily want to leave it behind because one gets to be twelve.

As a matter of fact, the Dome Kids, recognizing their own reluctance to "put aside childish things" forever, have structured a miniature Little Room of their own in their own domain. It is an island to retreat to, cushions, a guitar, record player, recorder, paint pots and drawing paper, treasured books and art objects; mostly like its original model, it is an ambiance. Come to think of it, people at LW are always evolving symbolic and sensuous Little Rooms wherever they are. Laps and pillows are ubiquitous. Practically no one of any age here has altogether given up his rights to love and be loved as a child.

As a rule, the Little Room readily admits older children when asked to. I rather hoped it would not do so with Donald. Donald would mean trouble. Donald is trouble.

He is a little boy for twelve. He has an agile mind. He is

alert, quick and he likes to control things. He is a manipula-
tor, both of situations and of people. His own group was beginning to resist him. Meeting after meeting had been called
upon him by his peers, and he was learning to use the meeting
as a useful device to try to maneuver himself into a position of
power. He was not making much headway with the Dome
Kids. No wonder he came knocking at the door of the Little
Room. I took a dim view of this ploy. Fortunately I was not
alone. In fact, my turn to express myself did not come until
midway through the meeting. Donna, ten years old, led off the
attack.

"Why don't you want to stay with your own group? You
have a Little Room in the Dome. What's the matter with
that?"
"It's not the same," was his evasive response.

Donna continued to remonstrate against his being allowed
to join, but a very quick proposal to grant him membership
emanated from what appeared to be the majority wing. Tension increased. Donna is a valued and beloved member of the
group, a day student, and everyone knowing this knew also
that the Little Room and its cohesiveness, its inviolability
even, meant a lot to her.

I raised my hand and was recognized by the chairman.
Understanding something of Donald's problems, I knew why
he needed the Little Room—apart from its supposed maneu-
verability. I knew why he might feel more secure there, why it
might even be good for him to be allowed to hole up for a
while in a place of relative safety. He had long ago learned to
cope, knowingly or unknowingly, with the intellectual tyranny of his highly cerebral parents. He knew how to assure

himself status at home simply by being the brightest boy in the class at school. He had not yet learned to cope with the equally tyrannical, although unspoken and unrecognized, demands of his own nature. He did not know how to secure love. He was bereft, shipwrecked without it. His needs, desires, his craving for affection so long unexpressed and unattended now almost literally cried out to be heard. To be heard and not to be hurt, for he was afraid, so afraid that he dared not touch others or let himself be touched.

Nobody could touch Donald. He walked alone in a place where others walk arm-in-arm, embrace and run and fight, throw punches and kiss and roll on the grass and in the snow together. Donald did not trust himself to be free. He did not even trust freedom. He was forever testing it, getting others— that is—to test it for him. Where were the limits beyond which one would get hurt again? He had to know, at others' expense, of course. For him the danger was too great. Understanding this, I feared its effect on the smaller children. Donna, for instance, was quite as vulnerable as Donald in another way, a more open way, fighting against any new element that might disturb and possibly threaten *her* safety.

I stated my position. It was—I admit—a careful one, a down-the-middle position, protective of both sides, yielding to neither. And it pleased no one, of course. "Let's let him come to classes here," I said, "if he wants to work and play in the Little Room during the morning hours. After all, classes at LW are supposed to be open to anyone who really wants to come. But after classes, in the afternoons and on the weekends and so on, I think the Little Room rights should belong only to the Little Room people and not to twelve-year-olds."

The democratic process is anything but easy, as I have had and continue to have seemingly infinite opportunities to observe. There are times when it demands a villain. This was one of those times. Those children advocating Donald's full admission now had their villain. Me. Those children who advocated his total exclusion also had their villain. Me again. The position is not uncommon or unknown to me. Not unexpectedly, I get a lot of children's anger and—in all fairness, a lot of their love also.

The battle raged back and forth, one child saying no, another saying yes, still a third suggesting a trial period as an alternative. Everyone was trying hard to be fair, to satisfy everyone and yet to keep the congruity and rhythm of the group intact. Finally a vote was taken and the motion passed to accept Donald as a full and participating member of the Little Room group.

"I won't try to lord it over anyone," the new member stated. "Or push people around. I really won't."

Did he mean it or was it simply his disingenuous way of stating precisely the opposite. We never had the chance to find out, for Donna promptly burst into tears and now a heretofore silent member of the Little Room group asked to be heard. He called a second meeting. Sandy often does this kind of thing, hears everyone out, makes up his own mind and then acts. He is nine.

Sandy said, "Donna still seems to be just as upset as she was at the beginning, so I think we ought not to let him in except for classes, after all."

A swift sort of consensus swept through the meeting. It was as though Donald had had his day in court and now Donna was to have hers. An hour had been spent in which the feelings of the outsider had been given major consideration. Now the process was reversed in favor of the insider.

"Would you mind very much," Donna was asked, "even if Donald was only in the class with you?"

"He's two years older than I am," Donna said. "And I'm scared he'd laugh at me or put me down if I wanted to ask Herb a question he already knew the answer to. So I'd be scared to ask anything like that."

We all assured her that no one would let him laugh at her or put her down or "lord it over" her or anyone else.

"Well, then," she concluded with wonderful—and irrefutable—logic, "it was passed earlier that he could come to classes no matter what. So I guess I'll have to accept it. I don't like it, but I'll do what I can with it because that's what was passed."

At this point the group seemed to feel that Donald's problems had received enough attention and that Donald himself had had enough "exposure." So they proceeded to demote him from the full membership he had enjoyed for the last fifteen minutes. The motion that he could only come into the Little Room for classes passed, with only one dissenter, swiftly into law.

ENTRY VII

"Do You Think White?" ended this morning. Not everyone came to class, and of those who did, no one came prepared. No one had done the reading. No one seemed to want to work.

Ten minutes went by. One of the boys, Brin, talked about Black Power. There was a little discussion. None of it was getting anywhere. It was another meeting, like the Little Room meeting, less formal and more manipulative. Teenagers are good at that, subtle and provocative. It was a beautiful cover-up, but I wasn't having any of it.

"If no one has anything to contribute, let's just drop the whole thing," I said. "Either face the fact that you don't want to work with this subject matter anymore and maybe we can find out why not. Or let's quit. If you all want to sit around and bullshit with each other, it's all right with me, but I'm not going to be a part of it. Maybe something has been going on in this seminar that's become too personal, too close to your own feelings."

"Like what, Herb?" Dawn asked.

"Like maybe the way the blacks are put down by society, for instance. Like maybe the way you are. What are your own feelings in the matter? Don't tell me about what other people think. What do you think?"

Silence. Finally: "What if someone reads aloud about Black Power, like Brin was talking about, and when someone doesn't understand, stop and ask for help?"

A chorus of "Yes," "Good idea," "How about that!"

The reading was short-lived. Looking around the room, I saw no one was listening. It was a cop-out.

"Look," I said, "if you really aren't interested, why don't you get off your dead asses and leave. You don't have to be here, you know."

A couple of students stayed on, but "Do You Think White?" was over.

ENTRY VIII

A mother brought her small son today for possible enrollment in the school. We had scarcely begun to talk when the lunch bell rang. Friday is allowance day. I officiate. The boy's eyes were wide with curiosity and delight as I invited them to join me in the main house to witness the proceedings. Then afterwards we'd talk some more, I said. There was room for him in the school. It was clear he wanted to come. We crossed the road together to the main house.

You push open the big front door. It swings to with a thump and you are straightaway engulfed. A simultaneous assault upon all your senses. Noise, motion, odor, warmth. The voices of children are shrill with joy and complaint, weave in and out of the clatter of dishes. There is a running and thumping of booted feet on the wooden floor, scraping of chairs, skidding of mugs across wooden tables to collide with pitchers of milk. Ceaseless noise, ceaseless motion of traffic to and from the kitchen. Pervasive—persuasive also as hunger begins to consume one—the warm smell of food.

Calls of "Herb" here and "Herb" there. Will you this and will you that? And when will you, or why can't you? And did you get my message, and will there be a meeting? And how about four-thirty instead of three? And what's for dessert and it's movie night, the committee chairman wants to make an announcement and a staff member has something to convey and there's somebody on the phone from New York.

And finally, fed, surrounded, everyone laughing, one begins to deal out the nickels and dimes, quarters· and half-dollars in the lounge.

An interruption. I feel a tug on my arm and turn to find a worried face looking up into mine. The mother, her boy grasped tightly to her side, says simply, "Good-bye, Mr. Snitzer. We're leaving. I don't think I want my son to have *this* much freedom."

The boy just looks at me. What is there to say?

Friday continued into the afternoon. Brin came to see me. He wanted to talk about the demise of the "Do You Think White?" seminar and he was enormously angry with me on account of it. He took what he called my put-down of the class—and of him—personally. He thought he'd done a good piece of work in his answer to *The Fire Next Time* and said he had not wanted to cop out. He still wanted to go on with the subject on his own. We scheduled a private class for the weekend.

I have feelings about it, but I forbore expressing them. Perhaps because I was tired. Perhaps because I was really discouraged about the failure of the seminar, Brin included, to come to grips with the problem on anything but a superficial level. Perhaps because I was the really angry one.

When Brin left, I began to think about the depth of my own involvement in the black scene. The American scene rather. The moral tyranny of a might-is-right ethic that tolerates if it does not in fact produce—black poverty, submissiveness, minority degradation.

A recent OEO meeting. Astonishment settled on the faces of most good citizens present when reminded that minority rights were supposed to be represented on the board. Who was a minority? There was a handful of World War I veterans still around. They'd be fine on the board. Black people? But they'd represent only one half of one percent of the county. One is torn between laughter and despair.

"Nothing human is alien to me," quoted George Groddeck in the *Book of the It*. Just that. It is the inhumanness of the society we live in and by and large accept that I am outraged by. The hypocrisy and the violence we do ourselves in open contempt for the democratic principles we profess to live by.

The whole idea of "Do You Think White?" as I look back on it originated with me. I triggered it, and people went along with me—part of the way. Motivation? Minimal. Be nice to Herb. Herb cares. Maybe there's something to it. Give it a try.

Might it not have worked anyway? Granted I started it, what stopped it? Truth might be that these youngsters cannot afford to look at racism for what it is, what it does—or tries to do—to the self-image of the black man.

They may be right to keep it at arms length, remote. The middle-class white teen-ager struggles to put together his own already fractured identity. His own fragile self endures similar anxieties and seeks to protect itself from similar defeats and oppression. Any fragmentation in others, any anxious search for intactness, for a way back from alienation, cannot be remote from him. It can only be painfully close and painfully relevant.

Kate came down the hill with Sigrid.

Twilight and sleepy silence enfolded us on the way home from Elizabethtown. Sigrid loves the supermarket, chewing gum and sunflower seeds. It has been a long day. Snow is forecast for the weekend.

ENTRY IX

The snow did not arrive. We had rain on and off most of Saturday and the prediction has changed to more of the same for most of the coming week. Brin was a no-show for his private class. Bob, however, did show for his. He has been pretty regular all term, trudging up the hill twice a week to tackle math with me. As he is inclined to plumpness, the trudge up the hill doesn't hurt him. The math class itself is something else again. It's an ordeal.

Bob is twelve years old and that aspect of his life which is visible to the naked eye he lives in the shadow of his mother's wishes. He has to, for if his mother does not approve, she cannot love. Her image of the boy Bob she does love may be very different from the boy Bob as he sees himself.

I might put it another, clearer, way. There is the son Bob

and there is the boy Bob. I am beginning, I think, to know them both. The son, plain for all to see, is a good and obedient boy who accepts the reality of his mother's statement that she knows what is good for him because she loves him. The other Bob lives a deeply buried fictional life. Hopefully it gives him the joys he is not yet strong enough to fight for openly.

Love that demands, that threatens, that needs to possess the beloved object—in this case a child—is a destructive love. It is, as R. D. Laing says, "violence that masquerades as love."

Bob's mother is not the only parent who feels that parenthood implies the right if not the obligation to determine her child's future as well as his past. For parents like this, a child's present does not exist. It is only a hiatus. It is a vacuum. Fill it with those experiences the better judgment of his elders choose for him. End result: the American Dream, the bright future of college, career, the steady climb rung after rung up the vertical ladder of success. Doesn't work out that way. Why? What's wrong? The child. The dream dies harder.

Of course it is not my dream and never will be. To require of any human being, child or not, that he be submissive if he is to be loved, acquiescent if he is to be accepted, conformist if he is to be approved of, is emotional fascism, a dictatorship of the heart.

It helps some children simply to be here, freed of many of the social and moral constraints demanded by the current scene, left alone to be. Just to be for a while. It frightens some parents. Unfortunately.

Bob is in his third year at Lewis-Wadhams. He still complies on the surface with the image of the good son. Perhaps he always will. But his private vision of himself has changed and is still changing.

Today nothing much remains of the anxious and seductive boy-girl or girl-boy he was when he first arrived, as though his flight into femininity had all along been a ruse necessary to secure his safety in the tightness of a family circle in which parental roles seemed to a marked degree reversed.

Bob's new charade is played quite openly. It is not sly or seductive. It is so barren of subterfuge that I almost suspect him of seeing through it himself, as though he were allowing me to catch unmistakable glimpses of his private role precisely that he may, with help, ultimately divest himself of it. I hope so, for the satisfactions yielded to him by the role of the "good boy" he now plays to a trusting entourage of little children are also ephemeral. To be all-powerful and all-good —he has been elected games master and wears the symbolic keys to the game room with honest pride—is still not the answer to self-fulfillment. How many layers to go? To be shed one after another like second skins. One cannot know. One can only guess. Wait, hope.

Bob lingered on after the lesson, as he often does on a Saturday, to play with Laura, our next to youngest, age eight. Kate had a fire going. Sigrid was making known her instant need for the simultaneous appearance of bottle, blanket and story as she clambered into the big fireside chair. Bob and Laura began the usual interminable and amicable wrangle about whether to play stud, draw or dealer's choice. Sounds of hammering reached us from the back of the house where at last the extension was on its way to completion—thanks to the thaw and ten days of mild weather. Lunch came and went and as the afternoon wore comfortably on it began to rain again.

Entry X

The rain was cold and sharp and blowy. I walked down the hill to my office, thinking of the long snowy months to come. The fall term will soon be over, a matter of three weeks or so. Already I have begun to feel the subtle changes in rhythm which mark the end of a term and the beginning of a holiday. Almost impossible to put one's finger on those first signs of tension and yet one feels them, hears them—voices go edgy or there are unaccountable silences, one sees them in children's faces, one experiences them—a week goes by with meeting after meeting called for the least provocation and sooner or later out it all spills like a ripped bag of marbles scattering its contents in a great, noisy, clattering confusion. New children generally don't know what to make of their own unease or anxiety. Those who have been with us awhile—like Craig—have less trouble getting their feelings out in the open. Is it in part that most children feel safety in ritual and distrust change? Or, as I am more inclined to think, abhorrence of change is itself only a symptom of the untrusting, unformed self. I am all right in here, says Craig. Will I be all right out there? In here, out there. Ought there be such a dichotomy?

Maybe there ought not to be, but in the world today that is the way it is. A young CO was waiting to see me in my office.

Several months ago we applied for and received limited approval from the New York Selective Service System to offer Alternative Service to conscientious objectors. The conditions for this approval are, for the most part, unexceptionable—that our enrollment not be restricted because of race or religion and that we agree to provide a continuous two-year work period. There is, however, a third condition: that we do not hire a CO—whatever his qualifications—to teach. We can hire him to haul the garbage, feed the chickens, mend the roofs, hoe the potatoes, prune the apple trees, shovel the snow and cook. We cannot hire him to teach.

The young man who came here looking for work knew this, of course, and had accepted it as a fact of life. He had no choice. Neither did I. Did he feel bitter about a system which tried to humiliate him because he had acted on the basis of beliefs rather than expediency? If he did, he did not say so.

He spoke of his background. He told how he was raised, a Baptist fundamentalist in the hills of Kentucky, and how he had got to college and had begun to read and think and look around him and to be appalled at what was happening to his country and to his friends, how he had lapsed from the narrow and fear-ridden religion of his youth and had turned against violence and hate and had become a Quaker. And a pacifist. He had taken time out of college in his third year to work for Vista. Then the draft caught up with him and here he was. He had heard of LW from a CO friend of his in California, who in turn had heard about us from another friend, another CO. And so it went. One became suddenly aware that submerged beneath the chaotic surface of today's "wartime" America another life on another premise is lived. I wonder how many young men like this one quietly go their own way, helping, supporting, advising each other on how best to salvage the two years demanded as ransom from them because their ideas are not the ideas of the majority, because they step to the sounds of a different drummer.

It is Bob's story all over again. A system of rewards and punishments. Do it our way, or else, says Uncle Sam, cart the garbage. There must be anger, I think, bitter and resentful anger felt deeply by even the most determinedly nonviolent among those who reject the military solution we are now committed to in Vietnam.

People are always saying with a shrug, "Well, that's the way things are." There was a time when "that's the way things are" meant the world was flat and the sun went around it.

The CO's name is Roger. He wears rimless glasses, has a soft brown beard and speaks with a slight stammer. He is slight and still brown from the Southern summer. He has brothers and sisters and subscribes to his hometown newspaper. He shows me an article about what Vista has accomplished back where he comes from, in a neighboring county, he says. Roger is twenty. We have room for him.

Entry XI

A course on religion, asked for by nine- to twelve-year-olds. Team-taught: Herb and Paul Berube. Outline and report: Paul.

An explanation of "primitive" religions and their evolution. The variety and number of religions around the world stressed. It was pointed out how recent all modern religions are in view of total span of mankind's time on earth. Few examples cited of religions once of major importance in Western world (Greek, Egyptian, Roman) which have now ceased to have importance to people in religious sense. Remainder of course devoted to study of major faiths in U.S. today: Protestant, Catholic, Jewish.

Primary purpose of course to involve students in discussion of their own feelings and ideas and experiences in the area of religion.

Early in course the kids were asked to write something about their own ideas of religion or some aspect of it. Caused a small panic. Reassurance to those who hesitated to risk writing anything without some clue as to what would be the "right thing" to write, the "right" answer. No such thing, we told them, as "right" or "wrong" answer expected. Just what you feel or experienced or think.

Some did write then, some waited, some wrote eventually, some not at all. Papers attached.

Excerpts:

I'll be a Catholic for today.

J. C. was god's son. Trinity. Resurrection. Rosary.

St. Paul—Augustine Fathers.

Infallibility.

SOUL   Heaven—purgatory-hell-limbo—free-will—salvation for unbelievers. Moderation—in food, sex, drink.

Sacraments. Chastity—for concentration on God. Vows.

Sin—sex pleasure outside of marriage, masturbation, cruelty to animals not really a sin, no immortal soul.

Censorship and movies. Communism, War.

[This paper is decorated in green ink with lovely ladies and a flower wreath.]

I have heard someone say that God started people off and gave us free will to do what we want and we should use our life well. That people must take care of themselves like we have policemen and that God isn't going to strike us down. I got this answer when I asked my Grandma why we have wars and she believes very strongly in God.

5. Death: Happiness but to some people death is scary and awful.

6. Life: People moving and doing things. And animals.

7. Heaven: No such thing, I don't think, and if there was I don't see how spirits get up to it.

God is an excuse for not being able to talk to other people. If you talk to elves and believe they exist, then they do.

God No image—Jewish God—invisible—like a spirit.

100 eyes—when he died
wasn't a We.

People like to die because they go to heaven or to hell but not many like to go to hell.
Some people like to go to heaven when they die
Be good don't swear don't steal or anything that's what good is
Be bad to go to hell I get mad at myself I wish I was dead so I wouldn't get mad at myself I don't like to die.

Some people think that God created the world. He was alone so he made the world and put people on it

Heaven has everything you want   it's beautiful   angels nothing bad
Hell there's devils and everything's all horrible the world is hell and heaven is heaven
heaven is up in space so people who have gone up in space ships should be able to get there.

Life for some people is the time for learning and growth, and life to other people is still learning but not growth. Life to all people is bad and good times. Sometimes when bad things happen you feel good but sometimes when bad things happen you feel upset and mad and hurt. . . . There are many many things in life that you go through. Like you get hurt and start crying.

THE LORD IS ONE

The catechism of the Jew is his calendar . . .

No perfect saints   Account for innocent
No original sin   pleasures missed
Sin—Missing the mark
Justly, Mercy, Humble   God forgives sins against Him.
Restitution. . . .

Entry XII

Thanksgiving began as another of those mild and rainy November days which can suddenly turn cold and treacherous, and did. Ice began to coat the branches of the trees and miniature icicles hung from the eaves. At two o'clock the power went out. A call went in to the power company and after two hours of inaction it was discovered we'd called the wrong company. Endless confusion up here between state, county, town responsibilities. By the time the right company arrived on the scene, only to tell us that our main transformer had burned out and it would be another two hours before power could be restored, darkness was fast falling. There was a great scurrying about for candles and the kitchen task force of Barbara and Margaret, augmented by Kate and Bunny Ring and a corps of ten children, set about preparing the feast.

A spirit of high adventure prevailed, the drama only heightened by the return to the school of a very shook-up group of two students and two staff who had skidded on the Northway coming home from a shopping trip to the village. Dave and Paul, who had been at the wheel, were both heroes. Paul, his head now swathed in bandages, had interposed himself between a child and the window as the car went into the skid and was quite cut about the head as a result.

The story was told and retold. Warm feelings flowed. Soon the tables were set, ringed by the children's flashlights. The turkeys were carved, the food began disappearing fast, and the toasts were well under way when the lights went on and a great cheer went up.

Not very much later, everything was cleared away, the tables pushed back and the dancing began. They danced until midnight.

Sunday, 1 December— Sunday, 8 December

ENTRY XIII

I have the flu and the unwonted luxury of three full days away from the school. A few visitors from down the hill have come and gone. Kate and Sigrid are away for the night. I am alone. The silence is complete and restful and rare. I play music, drink tea, read, fall asleep, wake up and begin the cycle all over again.

Here is Hermann Hesse, rediscovered, and I am again moved by him as *Steppenwolf* first moved me deeply a long time ago. From *Beneath the Wheel*:

> Teachers dread nothing so much as unusual characteristics. ... A certain streak of genius makes an ominous impression on them, for there exists a deep gulf between genius and the teaching profession.

and

> Anyone with a touch of genius seems to his teachers a freak from the very first. As far as teachers are concerned they define young geniuses as those who are bad, disrespectful, smoke at fourteen, fall in love at fifteen, can be found at sixteen hanging out in bars, read forbidden books, write scandalous essays and occasionally stare down a teacher in class. ...

Reflecting upon the school world of Hesse's time and on the motivations of teachers, I find my mind wandering inevitably to one of the problems which never ceases to be of underlying concern to us here. Again and again Kate and I confront it.

The idea that man can attain to earthly paradise—a Utopia—appears over and over again in the history of Western thought. (Nirvana is something else again, isn't it?) Something of original innocence and beauty, gentleness and wisdom is longed for:

> . . . to see in imagination the society that is to be created, where individuals grow freely, and where hate and greed and envy die because there is nothing to nourish them. These things I believe, and the world, for all its horrors, has left me unshaken.

Bertrand Russell's words were the jumping-off place for one of the most successful seminars we have had. We went backward and forward in time, dipping into a variety of cosmogonies from Plato to Rimmer, with the final outcome that children wrote their own notions of how human society might be improved.

Some were fantastic:

> Marl is a utopia set up in a cylinder, most of which is under the sea. Some of the cylinder sticks up above the water and under a Dome of plastic are the farms of Marl. I live in Marl with Barb.

Some quite practical:

> My utopia is a community of about 75 people living underground. . . . [Footnote: Almost all Utopias seemed to include the notion of physical separation from existing society, under or above the sea or earth.] There are plumbing and sewage systems. Nearby are woods, fields, water supply and an organic garden. We sustain ourselves by crafts . . . which we trade or sell. The money is held by a few chosen officials. Most of us are vegetarians. Some buy meat in town which is nearby. The town has a hospital, we have one dentist, two doctors and four analysts. We like to know about ourselves.

Some Satanic:

> The land of Magi—my anti-Utopia—exists as a kingdom on another planet, ruled by me the Grey Witch.

Some idyllic:

> What's most important about the utopia is that it cares about feelings, human feelings, and it wants to free them. The most beautiful thing about our love in the utopia is that we are creating care. We will have happy children. . . .

With the marvelous logic, poignant in its directness, of children, almost everyone's Utopia included bits and pieces of the Lewis-Wadhams world they do in fact live in.

I like to think that the "Utopian" nature of this world is not Utopian at all, but rather the reflection, in children's terms, of an environment that allows children to experience childhood. A child in a child's world needs to feel that he is a human being in his own right, not an appendage of an adult world where his own priorities count for little. He needs time to grow. He needs time and freedom to find out for himself about himself, and he needs to be able to do this without fear. He needs security, warmth and protection to enable him to express fully his desires and hopes, joys and loves and pains. If—that is—he is not to forfeit in the process of growing up the essence of himself, his life-force—call it what you will—the ability to feel, to accept life, to consider it worthwhile.

To say that Lewis-Wadhams exists to help provide children with a continuous experience of freedom and democracy in childhood is not to deny the existence or the exigencies of the adults who support them and who are an integral part of Lewis-Wadhams. However, it is a rare adult who has experienced the freedom to be a child in his own childhood. And so it is a rare adult who is not tempted by what he finds here to relive his unlived childhood, to regain some of what he has irretrievably lost, to be loved as a child again, warts and all. Of course, it does not work out that way. We are not Utopia, and no adult can become a child again; much as one or the other of these fictions might appear desirable, or even attainable, they are not. And here lies the source of much of the misunderstanding which plagues us in our relationships with teachers.

Andrew, a young man who used to teach here, came by for a weekend visit and hearing I was laid up paid me a sick call. We talked of this and of that, former times, the school, other staff members, students, the loveliness of fall in the North Country and how he had missed it, and now with winter around the corner he was on his way even further north where he had hopes of starting a school of his own. It seemed a vague sort of plan. Andrew did not elaborate and I did not press him. Both of us, I think, knew that his chances were slim and his qualifications open to doubt, not academically perhaps but . . . "Troubled children, you know, Herb," he was saying, and I did know, as did he, that it was himself we were talking about. He mentioned how Lewis-Wadhams had changed him, and this I knew too. I had witnessed the change, as we witness the change in almost everyone who comes into this community. It is bound to happen. Freedom is a heady notion and a contagious one. Only the exercise of freedom on an adult level is hard to come by.

The feeling of fulfillment rarely lasts, and the disappointment can be cruel. Sometimes a flood of tears, sometimes anger exploding unexpectedly at a child, at another staff member, at me, is self-revelation. Sometimes everything comes to a dead end, a full stop, as with Andrew. He could not get past the rage that overcame him. Nor could we get through it. He felt betrayed. He refused to believe that Lewis-Wadhams had not let him down, that he had not been victimized by Lewis-Wadhams but by himself.

Andrew was one of our first staff casualties. I wonder if today, four years later, we would be able to do any better for him and for ourselves. The children, even those who had been closest to him, rarely talked about him after he left—the younger children, that is. Among some of the teen-agers, however, it was a different story. There were angry questions about why he had left, whether I had asked him to go, and if so, by what right had I done so.

The departure of a teacher for whatever reason usually is disturbing, even divisive. There are rumors. Sides are taken. My role as director of the school comes under attack. Is it—are we—really a democracy after all?

Entry XIV

On reading Ashley Montagu's *Anthropology and Human Nature*. He says:

> The ethical principle of equality does not depend upon the biological findings of scientists, but upon the simple judgement that every human being has a right to the development of his potentialities by virtue of the fact that he is human.
>
> It is strange how often one hears it said that equality will eliminate differences among human beings. The contrary is, of course, true. Equality maximizes, inequality minimizes differences.

Entry XV

Sunday evening. The wind is really blowing now and the snow, which has been coming down steadily since early morning, is beginning to pile up in drifts against the house. Helping me feed the fire has become a new source of joy for Sigrid, as has helping me knock the snow off my boots when I come in from the woodpile.

Back in school this afternoon for the first time in several days I was, once more, made aware of the extraordinary change in rhythm which marks the term's end. People are edgy. Some know why and some do not. People are always calling meetings on each other. The smallest incident calls for fanfare and alarums. "He came into my room without knocking." "Gloria wouldn't turn down her record player even when I asked her to at least fifty times." People are stealing from the kitchen. "We're hungry," they say. Hungry for what?

The dynamics of hunger can be vastly oversimplified. Some children are always hungry. Missing snack time for some can be disaster. A couple of boys out biking beyond permissible limits will phone in, risking discovery of their lawbreaking, to say that they may be back late and please save some supper for them. Because inordinate hunger and the stealing of food are always exacerbated at the term's end, it is tempting to think of these as largely motivated by the simple fact of facing home again. That the need to fill up is a hedge against want is plain enough, but want of what? Love, security, warmth, being cared for—all these things, I think, and more. In a little child, with his time sense still limited to the hours between sunup and sundown, the existence of tomorrow still fairly dubious, and the existence of next week hugely theoretical, the response to a change in ritual can seem devastating.

Some of the commotion going on here before a holiday, involving children of any age, can be understood in similar terms. "What's going to happen next?" they are asking, and this is a double-edged sort of question. For it means, how will things be at home, will one be loved and cared for and welcomed there? And it also means, how will it be at school when one gets back? Will it be unchanged? Can one find one's place again as before?

A little girl of ten said when I brought her back from the station after a spring holiday and we rounded the bend in the road, coming in sight of the school buildings, children on bicycles, a few staff members sunning on the new grass: "I didn't believe it would be here. I didn't really believe it till right now."

I think this is part of a child's vulnerability, part too of his feeling that he is being treated like a "thing" again, told that now it is time to leave and that one is not to come back until told to—until, that is, one is wanted again. An ugly thought, and once more the matter of freedom of choice, the right to live one's own life, is discovered to have limits, reasonable limits perhaps, but no less uncomfortable to live with for all that. In any case, whatever the complexity of responses may be to the knowledge that the end of this coming week means the end of the term, it is better by far that these feelings be allowed to surface, no matter how many meetings this surfacing entails, no matter how apparently insignificant the beefs, how apparently reasonless the hairies. Artificial though the distinction may be between school and home, arbitrary though this compartmentalization may appear, seeming to some an unnecessary interruption in the life-process, it is only one of the many frustrations, natural or unnatural, one is going to be faced with in "real life."

It occurs to me that those who fault a "free school" like Lewis-Wadhams for failing to "teach" a child to deal with frustrations are those who think that accepting frustration—

i.e., being grown up—means denying its existence. On the contrary, to my way of thinking, nothing is to be gained by denying the existence of one's frustrations, everything to be gained by recognizing them and being helped in one way or another to do something about them. The something one can do is as often as not merely a matter of getting out (or at) how one really feels. For this one needs a lot of support.

Tim is one of the older boys, fourteen, in his second year here, and he has been having a terrible time of it lately. There is scarcely a law he has not broken. He has been making a general nuisance of himself, not only to others but to himself. He looks like hell, strained, anxious, and I know he has not been sleeping, breaks into the kitchen at all hours, steals food, clumps up and down the stairs most of the night, knocking things over on his way to and from bed. He is an ungainly, tall, thin boy. One of those youngsters who appear to sprout rather than grow, in a variety of assorted directions all at once, his too-long arms and legs seem about to come unstrung at any moment from the rest of his body. Altogether he himself appears to be about to come unstrung, all knees, elbows, skinny wrists and too-large head on too-thin neck.

He is perched like an awkward young bird in acute discomfort on the library table.

Tim: Look, people, I break into the kitchen because I'm hungry, goddammit, can't you dopes understand that?

Voice: Sure, but you've got money.

Tim: What's money got to do with it?

Marti: Go down to Dot's Diner and buy food if you're hungry.

Tim: Jesus Christ, that's some solution. Who is going to give me a ride to Dot's Diner every time I'm hungry?

Mimi: Well, look, you know you're always hungry, right? So, why don't you put in some supplies and cook for yourself, like in the teen house kitchen. Nights, you know, any time you want to. Midnight. Who cares? Look, you don't have to steal to get fed.

Tim: Some fun, fixing myself a little midnight supper in the teen house.

Brin: Yeah, some fun, like shooting off fire extinguishers, like you did yesterday. Like that's fun, right?

Tim: Boy, how stupid can you get? Sure it's fun.

Craig: Look, Tim, we're only trying to help, you know. Every time someone opens his mouth you are ready to fight. That's no help.

Tim: Well, then, fuck off and leave me alone. I don't know why I do things all the time. How do I know why I do what I do? I just do it.

Cara: Okay, so you just do it, and in doing it you make life unbearable for other people. Like me, for instance. The last week of the term is rough enough without you making it worse, at least for me it is.

Bob: You're not the only one. Look, the last week's the last week, you know. We don't always want to have to think about you and what you're doing to fuck it up for everybody. I've got my own thing to think about. In a couple of days I'll be home and you know what that means.

There was a lot of laughter, but it did not ease the tension the way laughter sometimes does, and the debate continued. Some went right on trying to make it hard for Tim, not willing to let up on him at all. They were making him a scapegoat in the classic sense, making him bear the burden of their own anxious and angry feelings. Maybe you guys want to be doing just what he's been doing, I wanted to say, particularly to a couple of the ten-year-olds who I knew damn well would have loved to have been able to flout the law the way Tim was. Others were really trying to help. They were not having much luck. I thought about how I would feel if I were Tim, heading for home in a couple of days, to be a "nobody" again. At fourteen it's awfully easy for a boy to feel like nobody, especially in a house full of females. Tim has an enormously practical-minded mother, three older sisters and a father who is absent most of the time, even when he is present—an imaginative, highly successful, committed scientist and the epitome of the absent-minded professor.

Tim, though he might feel he counted for nothing at home, was at the moment busy making sure he counted at Lewis-Wadhams. He was quite the center of things, and his truculence dared one to try to dispose of him easily, with difficulty, or at all.

"There's nothing to do around here." He glowered. "Like, maybe I'm bored."

"Bored with being you?" someone asked. "I'd be bored too, being you."

"Then maybe he'd like to be me for a while," I said. "Tim, you want to be director of Lewis-Wadhams for the next few days? It's anything but boring. How about it?"

Someone took a head count. As over two thirds of the school was present, the discussion period was voted into a meeting, at which this proposal received formal hearing. I defended it against the groans of some of our more law-abiding citizens.

"Among other advantages to all of us," I said, "is that if he wants the job and takes it seriously, he couldn't go on breaking the laws he's supposed to uphold, could he?"

"Oh, couldn't he though. That's what you think," from one of the ten-year-old outlaws, a would-be Billy the Kid! Jerry Rubin? Abby Hoffman?? Robin Hood???

"No," said Tim. "I wouldn't do that. Not if I took the job, that is."

In the fairly short natural history of Lewis-Wadhams, although this is the first time I have suggested my own temporary replacement as director, it is by no means the first time I have been temporarily displaced. Some occasions have been stormier than others.

Five years ago all government was quite simply voted out of existence, the move to anarchy spearheaded by a group of eloquent and angry teen-agers who saw in the new—to them —notion of freedom a way of avenging themselves for all the ills they felt had been visited upon them in the past. We were a new school then. The chaos was disastrous. Only the Little Room survived, continued to uphold "democracy," defied the majority decision, went right on holding meetings and passing laws.

Scarcely less dramatic, although considerably less damaging, was a subsequent overthrow of the democratic system in favor of a benevolent dictatorship. A monarchy, it was decided—a limited monarchy, that is, with existent laws remaining in force to be administered by a King—would be more efficient. Democracy was too slow, said the newly elected King Remo. He would administer justice quickly. He could always be overthrown if people didn't want him anymore. They could always pick a new King. Things went along smoothly for a while until the King was confronted with two young lawbreakers found in possession of explosives. A serious offense, the penalty was expulsion. (The unusual harshness of the law against possession of firecrackers has a history, dating back to the time the Northway was under construction and a couple of children were discovered trying to light a stick of stolen dynamite. The science teacher called a meeting and explained what would have happened had the attempt been successful. The meeting went all the way and voted expulsion for anyone who fooled with any explosive of any kind, including firecrackers.)

The King found the law anachronistic. There was, however, in the absence of a self-governing and law-making mechanism, no way to amend it. He didn't have the right to strike it from the books. He only had the right to pass sentence. He did so, after confiding his doubts to me about the wisdom of a kingship after all, the burden of responsibility weighing heavily on his shoulders. He decreed that the two guilty parties be suspended for two weeks, that they remain on school grounds, be permitted to eat and sleep on school property, but be deprived of all other privileges of membership in Lewis-Wadhams. Then he called a meeting and abdicated. Democracy once more became king.

Finally, also in the early years of Lewis-Wadhams, two boys of ten and twelve got themselves voted dictators. A day and a half of their tyranny was enough. They were pronounced bastards and voted out of office.

"What if I did take the job, Herb," Tim said, looking at me directly for the first time since the meeting had been convened to consider the proposal to make him pro tem director. Instantly a score of voices were raised demanding to be heard. The chairman cut through the din, peremptorily ordering everyone out of order to shut up or get out. "Tim has the floor."

"What if I do take the job, Herb," Tim asked, "what will my duties be?"

All heads turned in my direction.

"Well, if you want the job, Tim, it's like this. For the next three days there'll be a lot of arrangements to be made for people to get transportation home, money . . ."

General chorus of laughter. That was it. The mood had swung over to Tim's side. He wanted the job and they gave it to him. Tim did not try to hide his feelings of pleasure. He looked like a boy something important had just happened to.

Monday, 9 December—
Saturday, 14 December

ENTRY XVI

Cold really hit the North Country this Monday morning. Twelve below zero when I awoke; the wind down, the sun out and a patina of ice glistening on yesterday's snowfall.

Ten o'clock in my office. Mary Tur, Tim and I confer over the last week's schedule. A batch of checks has arrived to be cashed and distributed for transportation home. I leave Tim and Mary consulting time tables, making telephone calls, arranging to get to the bank in Elizabethtown, scheduling meetings with the End of Term Party Committee and so on.

ENTRY XVII

A retrospective. The last week is over. The term is over. It is Saturday, quiet in the school this evening and nearly empty.

All of the children and all but a few of the staff have left. Most have gone home for Christmas. Some have gone to visit relatives or home with a friend. A few really have no home, not necessarily in the sense of their being orphaned or minus one parent or the other, but in the sense of home as a place of warmth and affection, a loving place. These are the children with whom we make the least progress.

We cannot make up to a child for the absence of parental love. Sometimes I wish we could, simply adopt them, that is. And sometimes I know that they want to adopt us, have us be home and parents and are very angry when this does not happen.

What we can and try to do—hopefully a sounder, although a slower kind of answer to their very real feelings of bereavement—is to help these children get through the helpless and useless rage they are consumed by. Justified as a child's anger may be against those he feels have rejected him or use him to their own ends, it is a poor source either of comfort or of strength to him. He has his own life to live, we say to him, and say it in a multiplicity of ways. What is past is past. Whatever one has suffered in the past on account of one's parents' way of life or values or choices has happened. It need not continue to happen. One's own life can begin. One can begin to find out what one's own way of life or values or choices will be. One need not be imprisoned, locked into feelings of anger, of blame. One cannot change what has happened. One may not be able to change one's parents. One can change oneself, one can—rather—discover oneself.

It is not easy.

Hardest of all to face up to for child or adult is the absence of an absolute answer. Americans particularly seem to need to believe in absolutes. Living and working at Summerhill, I learned a lot about myself: Herb Snitzer, individual; also Herb Snitzer, made in the U.S.A., cultural product of the relentless American search for something we like to call "meaningful existence," also for something we claim as a birthright, name easily but live rarely—freedom. And happiness, of course. I began a long time ago, first when my personal unhappiness led me to seek therapy, and later at Summerhill, to wonder if we really understand what is meant by any of these concepts, not as concepts but as possible living realities.

Neill says it this way:

> No one can be entirely free. . . . What we mean by freedom is inner freedom. . . . Children are innately honest, and they expect you to be the same way. It is one great thing about childhood. They are open and honest, and if allowed to express freedom will remain this way all their lives without the shutting up of their feelings towards others. They won't be afraid to love someone. . . .
>
> Living should be for itself, not for money, not for success, not for Cadillacs. . . . Now, nobody can be happy all the time. . . . By happiness I mean a sort of feeling that life is good in the main, that you are enjoying life without hating and struggling with other people to get something. . . .

Neill was in New York this week. It was good to be with him again. I felt many wonderful things just talking with him on the telephone the morning he called. Memories filled me, of the warmth and fullness of life lived at Summerhill; life lived, not bypassed. Only by a handful of people, if you will, as we here at Lewis-Wadhams are only a handful of people. Scarcely enough to change the world, some jaundiced critic would sooner or later find it his bounden duty to point out in those days. Even in these days when the atrophy of the ability —or the freedom—to feel, to be, to know joy, has become apparent to many, many Americans, the notion of children experiencing freedom as part and parcel of the learning process has not gained much more than theoretical "credibility." It is practiced more often in the lecture hall than in the classroom.

Central to my memories of the days I lived and worked at Summerhill is the "Old Man" himself. A. S. Neill was nearing eighty then, a steady and supportive presence in that loving world, a tender presence for all the sense of indomitability the man gives off. Everything about Neill tells you that he who loves life cannot be beaten by it, that strength is not all muscle, it is also warmth and tenderness, an embrace and it is laughter. I have met few men as wonderfully alive to those about him as he is to himself.

Kate and I drove into New York to see him. Snowy fields, icy roads and early winter darkness drew us close. Kate had never met Neill. Neither—except through the pages of a book I had written—had the Lewis-Wadhams children. Stranger though he was, clearly to everyone up here he was both familiar and beloved, for we were entrusted to deliver to him an invitation to the End of Term Party. It was a five-foot scroll. Everyone's signature was on it, and it was bright with decorations, flower children's symbols of love and affection. The feelings in the school were electric as Kate and I set out. Joy was there and hope that we would bring him back to school with us.

Neill looked tired but his vitality seemed undiminished, his handshake as resilient, his eyes as alive, his forthrightness as undisguised as ever.

"Ah, Herb, it's good having dinner with the two of you," he said. "You don't ask me such bloody fool questions all the time. Everyone always asks me the same fool questions and I always give the same fool answers. Or do I? I wonder? One is always being quoted to oneself and asked what one means by this or that, or does one still mean it, and what does one think today and so on. I'm tired of it. Perhaps fame at eighty-five is not what it would have been to me thirty years ago, or," he added with a wry smile, "what it would have meant to Summerhill thirty years ago."

"And to the world of education," I said. "Yes," he said, "perhaps."

We talked for a bit about the struggles he had had and was still having to make a financial go of Summerhill, still having to go about on lecture tours—as this one to the United States—to make ends meet in spite of the fact that his writings are now widely read and his ideas widely discussed, if only beginning to be understood.

My love for Neill has not diminished, nor my respect for his accomplishments of the past fifty years. In the six years we have run our own school I have met many of the situations Neill has had to confront time and time again. We veered away from talk of the economic struggle and began to speak about the day-to-day situations one is faced with—requiring strength and clarity and more—situations which can be honestly faced and worked through only if one's feelings of love and respect for children are real. One's own inner responses are not always easy to recognize and to confront—responses to people, parents, children, staff, one's responses to life and to death, one's own anxieties and one's own fears.

"Death holds no fear for me," Neill said. "I'm not afraid of dying, you know, just of not living anymore. That's it." And that was it, I thought, a summation of a man's vitality, seeing life as a good thing to have and wanting to hold on to every bit of it.

We got back to Lewis-Wadhams, Kate and I, barely in time for the party. Neill's absence was a disappointment. Three students were waiting to receive him in our living room. There was a fire blazing and a kettle boiling for tea. The committee looked crestfallen.

"He wanted very much to come," I said and stopped. The fragility of the old, of the young, of life itself I thought about. The fragility and the toughness, I thought, and did not know what else to say.

INTERIM

Sunday, 15 December—
Wednesday, 8 January

Entry I

Christmas has come and gone, arriving in the wake of a blustering Nor'easter that blew down upon us early that first Sunday morning. The commotion of the winds and the whip and sting of swirling snow lasted two days, slapping against our windows, seeping in here and there through chinks and crevices, and sliding across the floor under the back porch door, tearing at faces, clinging to gloves and boots and necks and ears of anyone volunteering to make a periodic foray to the woodpile.

Then in a long night the storm blew itself out. A strange quiet afterwards. Not unwelcome, but eerie. A feeling of remoteness after nine—then ten—then eleven o'clock bedtimes over, a last rock record, a last story, the flurry of giggles behind closed doors, the brief beginnings of a stillborn quarrel, trips to the bathroom, a dream and a hug, the midnight bottle. Sigrid sleeps halfway through it. The wind dies away. No breath disturbs the snow. The sounds of silence. Unexpected, unfamiliar, remote, strangely more clamorous than the din of wind, of children, of music.

Today, with only four days to go before school begins, the first of a series of pre-term staff meetings is scheduled for late afternoon. There is a lot to be talked about between now and Thursday, more than usual because of the new staff members: Dave Reuther and Louise King, Mike McCaffrey and Roger Davis, the young CO, who will be with us for the next two years on maintenance.

The teaching "credentials" everyone is always asking about are abundantly present with the new staff as with the old: college degrees, special skills—Louise in music and anthropology, Dave in English (an honors graduate of Michigan, followed by an instructorship in freshman English at Denver); Mike a B.A. from Fordham and a year in the New York Model Cities program. Of the "old" staff returning: Paul Berube, pre-med B.A. from Kansas State, followed by graduate work in philosophy, a teaching assistantship and a year in Vista on the Cheyenne Reservation in Montana; Bunny Ring, Massachusetts College of Art, Tufts graduate work in art education, art teacher in Newton public schools, set designer and singer with Boston Opera Players until two years ago when the Ring family en bloc—four children, horses, cats and talents—moved up here; Dave Hartman, three years at Lewis-Wadhams after two years in Rensellaer Tech, a year of study and teaching in Sweden; Jill Eckhouse, B.A. Syracuse, Bank Street College of Education, two years of tutoring and observing in Syracuse public schools, a French prize winner of Alliance of French Teachers, Midwest; Julie Hickson in her first year here as apprentice teacher in the Little Room, but her fifth year of residence at Lewis-Wadhams where she came as a student at fourteen, four years ago.

There are other kinds of credentials needed to teach at Lewis-Wadhams, but they are not so readily measurable, and in fact no amount of talking about them in prior visits, private interviews or in staff meetings really prepares a teacher for living as well as teaching in a "system" which compels no child to go to classes, expects no child to follow along a pre-figured path of orderly, graded achievements in order to emerge as an end-product of a certain and specified kind, and relies on democratic self-government to deal with the kind of day-to-day problems which traditionally culminate in a mute, tearful or rebellious confrontation in the principal's office.

The usual arsenal of small arms weaponry from which a teacher traditionally draws strength—a podium to stand be-hind, rows of desks for children to sit at, tests, rules, the mo-tivational goals of status, power, rewards and punishments—are missing in the Lewis-Wadhams classroom. There appear to be contradictions in what is expected of a teacher here.

He has not got a captive audience, and yet his job after all is to teach children. If a class abruptly deserts him or gradually oozes away, are they lazy little bastards or is he a failure? Automatic authority does not accrue to him merely because he is an adult, and yet children look to him for aid and support, for strength and understanding in a way he has not generally experienced before. He cannot "lay down the law," yet he is not expected to grovel before children, to woo or manipulate them. He knows more than they do about certain things, yet they feel free to challenge what he has to say. Also they are likely to be great question-askers. He is not expected to have all the answers, yet "because I say so" is unlikely to satisfy anyone.

What really seems to make the impossible possible in the

Lewis-Wadhams classroom is that child and teacher meet on terms of their inherent equality—dignity, if you like—as human beings, as persons. However older, stronger and wiser in the ways of the world the one, however younger, weaker and more innocent of the ways of the world the other, the liking each other or the liking of life itself, perhaps, is what really counts. Life, a respect for it and an awareness of the pleasures and bewilderments of simply being human, really forms the bond between child and teacher, teacher and child, which is at the root of the learning process.

Educating children (if indeed this is what happens) for a world that doesn't as yet exist seems more the work of prophets than mortals, but even though there is an overabundance of mortals and a dearth of prophets, nevertheless educating for a new world is the only way. Grammar, numbers, facts— what are these in light of the overpowering, all-encompassing desire for life and pleasure felt by every little child born through love? Life is fun and joy, discovery and adventure. How small the pains and heartaches seem when balanced against the desire to stretch out little hands and encompass the world.

The good teachers are those who know that life, in the main, must feel good or else all the grammar, numbers and facts are worthless. Educating for a new world is as much a discovery for the adult as for the child.

I think the best of the old-time teachers knew this. Sadly, they were few! No methodology or teaching machine can replace it. Who has not one childhood memory of the kind of teacher who said on the first singing summer day, when a whole new, lazing world came in the opened windows and no one could sit still, "All right, class, let's have our lesson outdoors today"? Under the tree, if there was one in the school yard, or out on the grass, or simply sitting in a circle on the hot cement, smelling the tar and grabbing for flies as one did the "nine" tables or the capital cities or struggled through the parts of speech. One teacher, out of years of schooling. A treasured memory. A sad comment on schools and teachers.

Looking back, I can remember too the teacher whose whole classroom life was a series of altercations, who could not "keep order," and everyone knew it, delighted in it, took advantage of every turning of her back, straying of her attention, to pass notes, make noises, throw spitballs and ask to be excused to go to the bathroom. Why?

Are children naturally cruel? *Vide The Lord of the Flies*, they spy out vulnerabilities and pounce, playing a sort of cat and mouse game. Would this sort of game ever have come into being if there had not been in the first place a kind of competition set up in the classroom between child and teacher, as well as between child and child? The orthodoxy of the classroom, its rituals, dogma, the sacred invulnerability of "Hey, Teach!" was not invented by children but by adults. Not unexpectedly, it offers itself as a prime target for any reasonably healthy, spirited child not already cowed into total submission.

A child's resentment against classroom orthodoxy is by no means ancient history here. Almost every child who comes to Lewis-Wadhams after a few years of Establishment schooling goes through a period of taking active revenge against us for past injuries. They will read anything and everything, for instance, except the books suggested in class or on a seminar reading list. They will write notes to each other, compose poems and letters and stories. They will cover the walls with graffiti, post notices on the bulletin board, but it is pure hell to try to get them to turn in "class" papers. Or they will simply not come to classes at all for a while. One little boy of ten jumped up and down in a fury saying he would never, never go to class and stopped up his ears with his fingers when I tried to explain to him that he was at that moment in a class—it was a math class in the Little Room. This was early on, before I myself learned, too late in this case, that it is senseless arguing with the way a child feels about something.

Talking and thinking about what it is that makes a "good" teacher here or elsewhere, I think when you come right down to it, the qualities of a good teacher are the same, no matter what the system may be. Teaching a child and teaching a subject may not be mutually exclusive, but with a young child in the beginning stages of learning, of growing and developing on a variety of levels more or less simultaneously, one is concerned with the whole of what is happening to him and within him, of which the acquisition of this or that skill, this or that body of knowledge, is only a part.

A difference between teaching at Lewis-Wadhams and teaching elsewhere may come down to the fact that the openness of the child-teacher relationship here, the directness of the interchange, the absence of the usual props and the simple fact of living together, with the necessity of establishing a relationship of which the classroom is only a part, causes not only the child but also the teacher to emerge in the round.

There is a high degree of visibility about the teacher at Lewis-Wadhams. People get to know him, and he them, in many contexts. He is not expected to be invulnerable, to be a paragon of virtue and patience, to be always right. He is known to be human, and if he has forgotten this himself, he soon finds it out all over again.

Sometimes he is able to deal with the often unexpected

ways in which this humanness shows itself. Sometimes not.
This depends not so much on the sum of his life-experience as
on the recognition, the insight, he is able to bring to it—to
who he is, who he thinks he is, who he wants to be.

Then, too, others may see him in a quite different light
than he sees himself. We live closely and inevitably respond to
one another on highly personal levels of perception and sensi-
bility. How any staff member may feel about another, or
about a child, or about me, or about how a particular situation is being handled, or about a school policy he disagrees
with, or about a problem of his own which is bothering him,
any and all of these personal feelings, reactions and troubles
can and often do affect the whole feeling tone of the school.
So we try to air them in special weekly staff meetings, on the
presumption that anything out in the open can at least be
confronted and—with the knowledge that we are basically all
supportive of each other—may possibly be solved.

Call it group therapy, if you like. These meetings can be
tremendous learning experiences. They are not always relaxed. We do not play games with one another. I did not
initiate these meetings, and when the idea was first presented
to me by a former staff member who had been a Gestalt
therapist, I hesitated, thinking that they might do more harm
than good and that if people had something they needed to
say, something which was deep within them, they ought to
seek help outside the school. We are primarily a school for
children, not for adults.

My position has not basically changed. I do not wholly
agree with Neill that, if ideally realized, the environment of a
Summerhill or a Lewis-Wadhams is necessarily a therapeutic
one in the full sense of the term. The needs of some are too
deep and too complex to be met by love, support, freedom

and trust provided by our environment. Some cannot even begin at the beginning, cannot accept the security that is a part of trusting in and being trusted by others. If this is true, as I believe I have seen it to be, of children, it is even truer of adults. Defenses acquire sophistication simply with the passage of time. Everyone has his own ways of handling his strengths as well as his anxieties, and how a staff member does so only becomes a matter of concern if it affects the way he responds to the children or if it disturbs others or himself.

Within the recognized limits of what we can achieve in these weekly meetings (and this includes suggesting professional help at times) the insights gained and shared—into the way we view people, how we feel about the culture we live in, the world we are all a part of and, most importantly, ourselves can be enormously supportive. No one need feel that he alone sometimes suffers a confusion of feelings or that he need hide what he is feeling from others—explosive, irrational, sometimes unbearably intense though these feelings be.

The expression of anger, however murderous, does not kill anybody. Tears of grief, pain, frustration, are not humiliation. Fear of failure need not lead to failure, or fear of love disguise itself as coldness. To show weakness is not to be destroyed—this, perhaps, the hardest truth to come by, to believe in, the slow but basic comfort of trusting others' humanness and one's own.

ENTRY II

More thoughts on the above—misconceptions about what freedom is. Freedom of choice, i.e., the ability to make decisions affecting one's own life, even if perfectible, reliable, would be no guarantee of freedom. Freedom (as personal dynamic) only evolves from one's feelings—feeling expansive, feeling open, feeling unafraid, feeling "good"—cannot be acquired like a new suit, drip-dry, wear-dated, or otherwise.

Educational environment, the "in" phrase, implies something one can participate in, can draw upon and give to, replacing the traditional word and notion of "school," an institution one conformed to, was controlled by. One was pushed around by it, manipulated; one shaped up or perished.

An environment which values persons as persons, not objects, respects freedom of choice, privacy and human differences, may reduce tension, lessen frustration, but does not in itself solve deep, personal, essentially private struggles everyone (child and man) experiences.

WINTER

Thursday, 9 January—
Friday, 17 January

ENTRY I

Everyone back from vacation. No new children. Hopefully, no new traumas. Winter is the longest term, the hardest, snowbound a lot of the time. A fire in the lounge's huge old fireplace always draws a large contingent of recumbent music-listeners, embers-watchers, story-readers, lovers. Little kids, cats, my dog are to be found more often than not in the kitchen pantry where laps are available, and in the vicinity of cookie-baking to be sure, and spaghetti and meatballs plus other favorites. "What's for lunch?" "What's for snack?" "I'm hungry, Margaret."

Notices on the bulletin board: "Charles is now called Mark." "Please call me Fleur," signed Linda. "My name is Cara," signed Susan. "George—Call me Sam." "Sally to be called Poppy."

You get so used to this you forget people's real names. Charles' mother called up yesterday evening to find out if he had arrived safely—a long trip from the Midwest involving

I I I

several changes. Charles is thirteen and absent-minded. He had arrived safely and was fine, but the person who answered the phone said he did not know any Charles. Enormous confusion. "Oh, you mean Mark," came finally. Name changes are taken very seriously around here.

Other notices on the bulletin board:

Ski trip scheduled as follows:
    Lv Lewis-Wadhams 10:00 A.M.
Instruction beginners Monday 4 P.M. back hill slope, etc.
    Louise King offers piano lessons.
    Bowling—Plattsburgh—Tues. 7:00 P.M.
    Film workshops, photo workshop—see Herb.

Announcement: Paul Berube at supper time bangs for silence. "Will all teen-agers who use the teen house for any purpose whatsoever [laughter] please meet with Herb, Dave Reuther and me [groans] tomorrow morning at 11 o'clock. Place—teen house."

The meeting. The teen house is an old-fashioned, two-story red clapboard farmhouse with a shingle roof and dormer windows. A number of smallish rooms on both levels are connected by odd passageways and a steep forked staircase. Kate and I lived there with our then youngest child, Laura, before we moved up the hill three years ago. It is a pleasant meandering sort of place and it is comfortable—a kitchen with a view of the valley, two bathrooms, plenty of bedrooms, a glass-enclosed sun porch of 1920's vintage and a square old-fashioned parlor. A towering pine shields its windows from the view of its neighbors in the staff house and the barn and from the road that passes within yards of the front door. We turned it over to the teen-agers after our hill house was built, to have a place of their own.

On the morning of the announced meeting it presented an appearance of utter dilapidation. Nothing was left of the furniture but one chair with a rung missing and a pile of sofa cushions on the floor. The kitchen had suffered similar degradation. The sink was clogged, the stove encrusted with grease, pots and pans blackened, dishes chipped. We had had meetings on the subject before.

"It's a shambles," I said. "What are you going to do about it?"

Silence. Mutterings. Groans.

Marti: "Just take the house back, Herb. Let the school have it back again. We can't handle it. We never could. It's stupid and humiliating to be supposed to when we can't. Nobody wants to. Nobody cares."

Outcry. Some people did care. Others sided with Marti. Marti is short for "Hamartia," the name Leslie assumed within weeks of her arrival at Lewis-Wadhams three years ago, a sophisticated, intense, remote and very thin twelve-year-old.

Marti at fifteen is a beautiful child. Thin, elegant, still remote. She has private ways of thinking and feeling which draw others to confide in her, as though her own singularity makes her responsive to the singularity of others.

All last winter she stayed in her room and listened to records and had private talks.

Marti: If somebody wants to take care of it, let them. It's not my concern.

Craig: Look, Marti, if everybody felt that way . . .

Marti: That's purely hypothetical, Craig. Everybody doesn't.

Brin: If she doesn't care, then what right has she got to enjoy it?

Sam: Or anyone else who feels that way about it.

Marti: I *don't* enjoy it. Besides, what have rights got to do with it?

Fleur: Well, I don't say it's rights necessarily, but would you like it if people left your place like a pigsty? After all, some of us happen to live here, you know.

[Fleur does. So do Craig, Brin, Sam and a couple of others.]

Jason (sixteen years old, mucho machismo): Like, so it's a pigsty. So what? So if whoever minds it that much, cleans it up.

Sam: Sure. Like, it's always someone else. Never you.

Berube: That means, as usual, no one. I thought all you people, not just the people who live here, wanted a place of your own. After all, there are only—how many?—right, six who live here out of twenty teen-agers. What about the rest of you? That's why Kate and Herb turned it over to you in the first place. They thought it would mean something to you to have a place of your own. You stated that yourselves.

Voices: They thought wrong. That's their problem. Who asked them to?

Tim: That's horseshit! Everybody knows it doesn't belong to us. Like, it's school property, it belongs to them, so why the hell should anybody care? I agree, it's their problem.

Brin: Tim, it's not their problem. I'm part of this school. The school belongs to all of us.

Craig: If you want to look at it that way, Tim, everything's their problem.

Sam: A beautiful cop-out, man.

Fleur: If he lived here, he'd care.

Marti: But he doesn't. Neither do I. Maybe it's your problem. You take it over.

Sam: Why not? I'm willing.

[General agreement from the six who live in the teen house. No demurrer from the others.]

Herb: If it doesn't mean anything to most of you to have a place to be on your own, where you can get away from the rest of us, be on your own . . . Are you saying that?

Jason: You're saying that, man.

Marti: Be fair, Jason. That's what we are saying.

Fleur: Enough rapping. Put it to a vote. I move that . . .

The resolution: only those teen-agers who agreed to care for the teen house and its contents will be allowed to use its common rooms—the lounge, the kitchen, the sun porch—at other than class times. It passed and took immediate effect. Everyone but the six who lived there left at once, with apparent relief.

"So be it," I said, a little downcast.

"What if they change their minds?" said Dave Reuther.

"You'll get used to that soon enough around here," replied Paul.

A couple of the little kids came up to me at lunch time and we had much the same conversation. When they got to be teen-agers, would they still have that law?

"When you get to be teen-agers, there won't be any 'they,' you'll be they, and you'll make your own rules, so don't worry."

A big hug. "I love you, Herb."

ENTRY II

Staff meeting first Monday of term. The new staff say nothing, watch, wait. The old staff plunge in.

X (to Y): I don't like the way you act with kids. It's like you're putting them down all the time. You're really rough on them.

Y: Why do you care how I talk to kids?

X: You scare them. It's scary to have somebody coming on so strong all the time.

Y: I wasn't aware of doing that. I don't think I come on so strong with kids. Does anybody else think so?

Z (to X): Why the *intensity* of your anger, even if it were true?

Y: You *are* angry, you know. He's right. Are you angry at me? You could tell me what you think about the way I handle kids without getting so angry yourself.

Z: It seems to me that you're angry at all of us. You look as though you think we're going to jump on you the way you say he jumps on kids.

X: All right, I am angry. So what about it? Bullying turns me off.

Z: You think he's a bully? Or do you think anyone's a bully who asserts himself with kids?

X: All these kids have had problems being pushed around by adults. Why should they get it here too? He's got that big voice and he throws his weight around. He's the authority and they've got nothing to say. They can't talk back. A kid's scared he can't talk back.

Here X's story begins to break down. No one agrees with what he has just said. If a kid is scared to "talk back" to adults when he first gets to Lewis-Wadhams, it's one of the first things he learns to do—with eloquence, obscenity and no consequences. What X finds hard to handle is his own anger at authority figures, his own fear of being "put down" by them. He is not alone in having these feelings. We talk about it at some length. How to rebel. Did one rebel as a child? Or, afraid to, did one quietly store up silent, futile anger?

Witness the enormous anger and hostility of current student revolts, the Sturm und Drang it takes at twenty to achieve independence of mind, spirit and—in fact—to be permitted to undertake the moral and legal disposition of one's own body. If nothing else were to produce this anger but the shock of recognition, it would be enough. Looking back on years of control and submission, one's own self-interest suddenly surfaces. It may be explosive. It is necessary.

> Student power is not so much something we are fighting for as it is something we must have to gain specific objectives. . . . The long range goal and the daily drive that motivates and directs us is our intense longing for liberation. In short, what the power movement is about, is freedom.
>
> Carl Davidson, SDS*

> We wish to take responsibility for all aspects of our lives. Because of this it is a power struggle. . . .
> Roger Alvarado
> Latin American Students Organization
> San Francisco State College*

> Autonomy is hard for some people to understand. It is only possible to understand when you don't have it.
> Student, University of California at Berkeley*

ENTRY III

The first week of classes ends today, Friday. All quiet. In

* From *Right ON: A Documentary of Student Protest*, by J. Naisbitt and M. C. Levine (New York: Bantam Books, 1970).

the morning mail, two invitations to lecture. One at Goddard College on "Sex Education in the Schools." One at Auburn Community College on "Children and Democracy."

Friday, 24 January—
Friday, 31 January

ENTRY IV

We talked at Friday evening's discussion about isolation. People have been going on about this lately, a certain group of youngsters particularly, saying they feel very alone and left out and don't really like anybody. Mooning around, looking bored and lonesome. I have been getting a rash of letters like that, notes saying people want to talk to me, feel abandoned, as though "nobody cares around here."

I take this partly at face value: the kids really mean this and feel this. Partly, I don't think they do. I think they are feeling something else. Feeling abandoned can be particularly true of new children, particularly true of children who come from families where they have been dependent, told what to do every minute, usually by an adult.

"If you're pretty much left on your own the way you are here, I can see that you might feel not cared about," I said. "You could interpret it that way. You might not quite know how to go about getting the caring-for you want. You'd also be likely to be suspicious, afraid to connect up with somebody else, somebody else your own age, for instance. Or if you were beginning to connect, that could be tough too. You might get clobbered. Maybe it's safer to go on claiming to feel isolated."

I started off saying some of these things. There was agreement and disagreement.

Herb: Like, it's cold out there and it's warm inside, and if you want to be on the inside, what do you do about it?

Donna: What if you want to go up to somebody and say you like them, and what if they don't like you back?

Sally: People don't always have to like you, do they?

Mika: You don't always know whether you do or you don't—like somebody, I mean. You start out feeling good with them and then it stops and you feel shitty again.

Brin: Maybe you'd rather feel shitty.

Tim: That's a dumb thing to say.

Marti: People have a right to feel alone, don't they?

Craig: A person can be alone because he wants to or because he doesn't know how to be friends with somebody. They're two different things.

Donna: Like what if I want to play solitaire and someone asks me to go for a walk. I don't have to if I don't want to.

Red: But what if you want to go for a walk with them. Do you? Or are you scared to? Or what if you play solitaire because you're scared to ask somebody to go for a walk with you . . .

Craig: Look, it's like maybe you don't believe if people say they like you sometimes.

Putting it down this way leaves out the spaces and the silences, as much a part of what is happening as what people say. There will be a silence, and then two or three voices at once break it. Some don't talk at all. Like Bob, who sits by himself and listens, and Jason, who stands up and walks around most of the time and pretends not to listen. Tim throws in his questions from the library table, where he perches cross-legged as usual. Craig has a girl friend. It started just before winter break. A tentative and careful friendship at first. Now one feels a rush of tenderness between them. Craig and Mika are always together these days. Red and Fleur are another new pair, a quiet pair, deeply protective of each other. Most of the time they keep to themselves.

Marti says she knows what I mean about feeling that one might be beginning to change.

Marti: Even if inside you feel different, it is easier to go on being who you were before. Like you feel helpless to do anything about it.

Craig: She knows someone wants to be her friend, but after a while she can't let them. If he's a boy, she closes the door on what he is feeling. She does not want to know it. So he fails.

Herb: No, Craig, he doesn't fail, the problem isn't his.

Nobody, finally, seemed to agree much on what isolation means, whether it means you like somebody and are afraid they don't like you, or you do not like anybody, or nobody likes you, or you just want to be alone, or you are beginning to connect and are afraid. We agreed it might be all of those things.

ENTRY V

Monday. Meetings seem to breed meetings; talk, talk; feelings, feelings. A certain feeling tone takes over, and for a while now that is what is happening around here. Winter terms are more likely to be like that. This one is proving to be no exception. The weather enforces togetherness. This can be cozy. It can also be terrorizing. Today is the thirty-fifth day of near-zero weather!

10:00 A.M.: Dave Reuther called a community meeting. He had been on "bedtimes" over the weekend. Both Saturday and Sunday nights people had been up until all hours.

Dave: I know I'm new around here. But I don't feel good about the antagonism directed against me by some of you people this weekend. Tim, Jason—you all know who you are.

I don't know what's bothering you older guys, but I don't think it's fair to take it out on me. I don't think it's fair to take it out on the little kids either. They need their sleep, even if you think you don't.

I felt put down by you little kids too. You bitch because we can't have a quiet bedtime on account of all the ruckus the big guys are making, but you don't back me up when I try to do something about it. I don't think that's fair either.

Cara (little kid): It's not fair to make the big kids get out of the main house like you wanted to. They've got a right to be there until it's their bedtimes.

Tracy (little kid): Look, Cara, they keep everybody else up. Is that fair? They've got their own dome to go to. Why can't they go there if they can't keep quiet?

Dave: If you were feeling that way last night, Tracy, why didn't you say so then? You just flopped around laughing.

Mika: Some people just get bitchy moods. They can't help it.

Dave: Well, all right. I'll accept that, but . . .

José: Maybe they think we got the black plague or something and so that's why we're not welcome in the main house.

Paul: I don't care about being in the main house. What's so great about that? At least in the boys' dome we got a right to stay up all night if we want to.

Jason: Some right. I agree with José. Who wants to sleep out in the middle of nowhere? Like, you're all uptight about us or something.

Many children have anxieties about going to sleep. The little ones like the house mother or the staff member who's on bedtimes not just to see that they're in bed when they're supposed to be, but to read stories, sing songs, play the guitar, have a last game of cards with before "Lights." Sometimes they just want someone to talk to, to give them a little special loving, a backrub and an extra hug or two.

The older ones are not so upfront about their anxieties— facing them or expressing them. This is particularly true of the lawless ones, the tough ones, the bullies and the loners.

I said I thought that the feelings that were coming out at this meeting were a continuation of the isolation we had talked about Friday evening. I also said I thought that had something to do with the way people behaved over the weekend. Nighttimes these feelings—of abandonment, isolation or just plain feeling alone and lonesome—could really get to you. The question is, what can we do about it?

Voices: Well, if some of the boys in the dome wanted to sleep in the main house, why couldn't they?

We could take turns, maybe, change around every term.

I'm not giving up my room.

Nobody said you, stupid.

Who's stupid, stupid?

Chairman: OK, OK. Shut up, everybody. Who wants the floor?

Herb: OK, maybe we can do that, shift some people around—whoever wanted to—and house Jason and José and Tim in the main house? Do you think that would solve it for the rest of you?

Although some of the older kids protested the possibility of moving while others felt it would be a good move, nothing definite came out of the meeting. No one actually said they would move into the main house. No one said they wouldn't, either. But within the next three days quiet once again returned to the little kids' sleeping areas. One of the more subtle characteristics we've noticed over the years is that sometimes things seem not to happen while a meeting is in progress, but one, two, three days or a week later the effects of the meeting or discussion are felt. This is one of those characteristics visitors have the most trouble with. They usually take at face value what happens in a meeting and sometimes are distressed when they "see" nothing happening. They leave thinking nothing was accomplished, while in reality things do happen, only by then the visitors are long gone.

Monday continues. Lunch. Staff meeting.

Staff meeting: We talked about the "crime of punishment," as Menninger puts it. Children who break laws, unreasonably annoy others, abuse someone's privacy, fail to return borrowed objects or disrupt community proceedings can be fined by majority vote at a school meeting.

Fines can be punitive or they can be supportive of a child's need. Children don't necessarily recognize the distinction: that whereas one fine may help a child over his difficulties, another will simply reinforce them.

A case in point: Lately Steve has begun to disturb everybody when the mail is being given out. He does not want to wait his turn and makes a scene about it. A meeting was

called on him and two quick proposals were made, one that
he receive his mail last, and two, that he have to wait an hour
after the rest of the mail is given out before he can get his.

He wants and needs the letters he gets from his mother,
who has been recently divorced, and all the old anxieties
come into play again. Would this mean another foster home?
He wants and needs her letters. Neither of the proposals
would help allay his anxieties. To the contrary.

I proposed that since for one reason or another Steve
seemed to need his mail first, he should be given it first.
Chorus of objections and it was voted that he get his mail
last.

The point is that the more insight staff have into a child's
needs, the more helpful they can be in getting children to
discriminate between a fine that hurts and a fine that helps.
This was not the case with Steve. Steve was a hard kid to
like.

We talked about the difference between the concept of
supporting a child and the reality of it. You may want basically to be on the child's side. Often you think you are, but
your own hang-ups get in the way.

We talked at staff meetings about tension and ways to
handle it in the classroom. It is no use trying to "translate"
academic material to a noncaptive audience with even one uptight child in it. Tension is contagious, particularly with little
children who express it directly. Ignore it and hope it will go
away? Talk about it? Comfort the child? Call a meeting on the
child? Make a joke of it? There is no prescription.

Knowing who a child is because you are around him most
of his Lewis-Wadhams life helps. We have very few day students, for that reason among others. Donna is one of them.
Sometimes she stays overnight. It is not the same, though. We
all know it.

Donna gets very upset when she's late for school, as she often is these winter mornings. Even cars balk at the ruthless cold of North Country winters.

She was near tears the other morning. We had just started to do "numbers" in the Little Room. It was about nine-thirty when she came in, bringing a little gift with her, as she often does. "Here's this beautiful little bottle I found," she said, "in the barn, of all places."

It was a beautiful little bottle. Everyone crowded around to see. I put my arm around Donna. She wanted none of it. There were a few drops of water left in the bottle. I upturned the contents over Cara's head. Cara is Julie's close friend. (She is also my friend.) "Herb, you shit," she said.

I knew what was coming next. Soon everyone was running to and from the sink, and the Little Room was laughing and shrieking and soaking. A change of clothes, hot chocolate for snacks, and the rest of the morning passed in peace and quiet.

After lunch Donna came to see me and we talked.

Donna: I'm always afraid I'm going to miss something when I get there late.

Herb: I feel what you feel, Donna. And you know I'm always here for you!

ENTRY VI

January ends. Nixon is in the White House. The Inauguration ceremonies—some ten days ago—contrasted sharply with my own mood. Along with many other Americans I am sure, I thought of Robert Kennedy on that day. A sense of mourning, of grief and of anger at his senseless and violent death. A sense of loss.

Robert Kennedy illuminated the issues that confront us, today more than ever, when power, status, control, and achievement, the four horses of the apocalypse, are riding hard.

David Schoenbrun says of *Thirteen Days*:

The myths of national sovereignty, the infallibility of experts, notions of vital national interests as distinct from the interests of all humanity, these are the political, moral and philosophical questions Robert Kennedy raises for all of us to examine. . . .

If we are to examine these fundamental truths in the broad sense, we ought also to examine them in the deeply personal sense, not only our views of the men to whom we give the power of life and death over us, but their views of this power we have given them and of life itself.

For some men the only meaning of life is power. To get it, to use it, *to keep it*. They are the dangerous ones. No longer in touch with their own humanity, they lose sight of the struggle that engages most men—to be able to live life, to live it quietly and openly.

Human, open, vulnerable, Robert Kennedy took no pains to conceal his private feelings behind a public face. Children, justice, grape-pickers, touch football, the blacks and students, Vietnam, his brothers, his family, his country—he cared about them all and it did not matter who knew it. Not afraid to be himself, he encouraged others to express their humanness as he did, and as does Robert McNamara in tribute to him. It is a bold and beautiful statement, rare in the political arena, of human affection for another human being.

"So it was," writes McNamara, "that I came to know, admire, and love Robert Kennedy. . . ."

I, too.

The theme of public posture versus what is really going on in a man's mind and heart continued to weave itself into much of last week's events, which I've not had a chance to write about until now.

Given the present social context, it is difficult for a besieged minority, ghettoized in Harlem, in East Village *barrios*, on Marlboro Country "reservations" or in migrant enclaves all over the U.S.A. to see relevance in the Lewis-Wadhams "experiment." The very word "experiment" (from which one day we will be free) connotes a test tube, implies tokenism. But whereas I hope we will shed the word "experimental," I know Lewis-Wadhams will remain radical all its life. "Radical" in the seminal sense of the word, as Martin Luther King used it to describe W. E. B. Du Bois's lifelong attitudes. That is, I hope we will be able continuously to explore and deepen our perceptions of what it is to be human, that we will be able to reach—to touch, feel, sense and liberate—man's potential for growth and joy.

If this seems at some remove from the day-to-day struggle of the black man to control his own destiny, I can only say that nothing is more germane to the idea of freedom—of revolution, if necessary—than to bring a child up free. Lewis-Wadhams is open to children and teachers of all backgrounds. We accept applications from the parents of nonwhite children on the same basis as we accept them from the parents of white children. There have not been many applications from nonwhite children and there have been none from nonwhite teachers. I regret this, and I keep trying to do something about it.

Last week I met with the director of a Harlem welfare center. Although not a black man himself, he has been closely identified over a period of years with Harlem's children and

Harlem's community needs and attitudes. He told me straightaway what I knew to be true, that before I could gain any
"credibility" in nonwhite communities I would have to break
through *his* image of what I represented—the white middle-
class Jewish liberal looking for token blacks to dress up the
"image" (that word again) of my white middle-class private
country school.

Yes, well then, let's begin to do just that, break down the
image. That is what I am here for.

After a while we really do begin to talk. We relax and the
talk grows heated and has point and is complex. We talk till
all hours in his remodeled West Side brownstone. A glacial
wind gusts up the side street from the river. Inside a great
fireplace. The smell of wood smoke, dogs (two), sleepy children (three), coffee, pastrami on rye, cheese, pickles, cigarette butts, wine. Talk, talk. Our wives join in. Children go to
bed. Dogs have to be walked. It goes on a long time.

In retrospect: a sense of unreality, as though this evening
would not be the time nor place to come to grips with "the
problem." There would have to be other evenings, with other
people, other places, other times. Yet we did, I believe, up to
a point get somewhere. Up to the point at which one says to
the other, "I'll see what I can do. I'll see some people. You'll
hear from me." I never did.

Some of what we talked about:

The need for the black man to democratize and to radical-
ize his own community. The school within this community,
the school his children go to, the quality of the education they
get, who teaches them and what and how become a focal
point, a battleground for survival on the black man's terms. If
you are going to say to the white man, this is where we live,
these are our lives and these are our children and our chil-

dren's lives, the school is where you are going to say it. The neighborhood school is where it's at.

For some blacks, that is. For others, where it's at is the middle-class Establishment school, public or private, suburban or urban. To the black teacher or the black parent or perhaps even the black child whose values are expressed in the current American culture, Lewis-Wadhams is only "rocking the boat." Competition for grades, the drive to be first in your class, to be called Mister and wear a button-down shirt when you get to be a teacher yourself, to be absorbed, assimilated, accepted within the system is what counts. To get ahead. Schools like Lewis-Wadhams by their very existence argue the incompetence, unfeelingness and irrelevance of this system. The Establishment-oriented nonwhite parent does not come looking for Lewis-Wadhams. Not yet. Pursuit of the American Dream has not yet become a nightmare.

We talked about money. Even if the inner-city child wanted to come to Lewis-Wadhams, could he afford to? We are not an endowed school, but we try to find ways to help children who want to come to us. Outside financial help is rare. Maybe someday . . .

We talked finally about roots. Am I asking black children coming to Lewis-Wadhams—or black teachers—to deny their roots, their culture, their blackness? I do not think so. A child is not asked to deny who he is when he comes here, but rather to be who he is, whoever he is.

I am not sure about roots, to what extent a child is rooted in a culture or a color, but if one takes a child's wishes, fears and dreams to be the branch and the leaf, the visible expressed sign of himself, then the "who he is" of a child appears to have little to do with the color of his skin.

When I first get up in the morning I feel fresh and it seems like it would be a good day to me. But after I get in school, things change and they seem to turn into problems for me. And by the end of the day I don't even feel like I'm young. I feel tired.   *Victor Y., age thirteen**

The question: How did you feel in public school classes?

"Boiled."
"Curtailment of interests."
"I got beat up all the time, frustrated."
"Something missing."
"Frustration and total confusion."

Walking alone around the park is just like forgetting everything. You see the free children playing. I remember I was a kid and I was always playing and dancing with the other kids. Life is easier when you are small. The parents, they care for you more and always give you what you want. I wish I could be a kid again. They hug you and carry you. When they kiss you goodnight or sing a song to you, you get so sleepy.

*Unsigned, age fourteen**

I have lost a lot of things . . .
I used to be very wise. I'm not wise anymore. I used to be pretty. I'm not pretty anymore. I used to love my life, I felt so warm I was just so glad to be breathing and moving. I used to feel so much more than I do now. When I was 12 I said Could I just feel so many things so deeply that it becomes so much that it would just stop feeling?
When I was 13, 12, I didn't know what I looked like. I know now . . .   *S. J., age thirteen*

I want people to care about me, to come up to me and talk to me, to show me warmth. I would like to be able to come up to people and be able to play or talk to people without getting

* From *The Me Nobody Knows: Children's Voices from the Ghetto*, edited by Stephen M. Joseph (New York: Avon Books, 1969).

uptight. I want to be able to have a say in things and feel like I have a say in things. In general I want to be more confident about things and have people see me and pay attention to me and know who I am and to feel warmth towards me.

M. R., age fifteen

I have felt lonely, forgoten or even left out, set apart from the rest of the world. I never wanted out. If anything I wanted in.   *Arthur Jackson, age fifteen**

When you get very mad at someone at a searten time, you push your lip out and roll your eye. Then you start picking on your little sister and brother and your dog and your friend. You do not want to eat your dinner.

Then you get mad at your self and you do now know what to do.

So you stop to apologize to your mother and father and your little sister and brother and your dog and your friend and you are nt mad anymore.   *E. J., age thirteen**

I really get mad at people who bug me. I don't say anything. I should yell your bugging the shit out of me. I get mad at adults a lot like at the Buget meating I was geting mad at any adult who said anything to me. I'm scared to get mad, I'm scared of what will come out of me.   *Unsigned*

People who hate their mothers don't necessarily have to be scared of their mother. It's not an unnatural thing. I use to think it was . . . I guess I come pretty close to hating my mother. I hate most things about her, but I love her. Something in me makes me love her. She's my mother, I guess.

Unsigned, age fourteen

Sounds:

Sounds can be curses or swares but are usually cunningly worded phrases that put down or rank-out somebody else.

* From *The Me Nobody Knows: Children's Voices from the Ghetto,* edited by Stephen M. Joseph (New York: Avon Books, 1969).

The best kind of sound is a corny sound such as "I went up to your house and asked for a drink of water and your mother gave me a bazooka and a hand-grenade and said . . . 'Good Luck.'"

Mothers play an important part in sounding. I don't know why but for some reason mothers are the subject of all sounds.

*Unsigned, age fifteen**

If I was a river or if I was a mountain or a forest or a hot fragrant island I would be a very paranoid existence. It really frightens me how much NYC has grown in just this century. In books you always read how there were farms in Manhattan and old pictures show the streets all covered with clean snow or treeish streets in the rain. Also graphs that show the population of the world doubling in no time at all. It really kills me that people don't wear gas masks in N.Y. It kills me how some people make millions and those people who work for them barely eat. The world is really crazy.

When it snows, I sit in the field covered by a blue blanket and I can count and look at each big snowflake until they pile up and melt into one another. But I am very lonely in the fields. And people get sick pretty soon of the same old you and you find that you get pretty sick of yourself too.

Unsigned, age thirteen

Progress limited:

> No trains stop here anymore,
> and the old train station seems
> to have become just a natural
> part of the landscape
>
> The shutters look as if they are
> cell doors, locking in our prisoner
> the past.

* From *The Me Nobody Knows: Children's Voices from the Ghetto*, edited by Stephen M. Joseph (New York: Avon Books, 1969).

133 «   WINTER

The platform's legs look exhausted
from the long years of supporting
a building which we once called
progress.

But, just as the wind must cease
to blow, so must we cease to exist,
and eventually we become a natural
part of the landscape.

*J. M., age sixteen**

"What makes you uptight, Jed?"
"It's hard to say, Herb."
"Okay, I know that, but try. Nobody is going to put you down."
"Well, I know that in public school they won't give you time to rest except during recess, and that's not enough time. Here I can rest when I want."
"What are you so tired about, Jed?"
"I'm just tired."

I am not like all the other children. I'm different because I like to hear birds singing but I don't like to hear people shouting. It is not nice to hear people yelling or shouting in the street.

Isaac J., age thirteen

Peter Abraham in *Mine Boy* says it this way:

Paddy: It is good to love one's people and not to be ashamed of what one is. But it is not good to think only as a black man. The white people in this country think only as white people and that is why they do this harm to you.

Xuma: Then I must think as a black man.

* From *The Me Nobody Knows: Children's Voices from the Ghetto,* edited by Stephen M. Joseph (New York: Avon Books, 1969).

Paddy: No, you must think as a man first. You must be a man first and then a black man. And if it is so you will understand as a black man and as a white man. That is the right way, Xuma. When you understand that you will be a man with freedom inside your breast. It is only those who are free inside who can help free those around them.

Saturday, 1 February— Friday, 7 February

Entry VII

A long, quiet weekend, cold, but no fresh snow. Everyone stays indoors most of the time, then on Sunday a long walk down to the bridge over the river at the foot of the hill. Ice and silence except for the creaking of the wooden planks under our boots as we cross to the middle of the old bridge, look down at the frozen water and dark, snow-drenched pines and talk about when spring comes.

I have been working on next weekend's talk at the Goddard Sex Education Conference. They wrote asking me for a title. "Sex Education Is Life Education," I wrote back.

The adult who thinks his job is to prepare children for life should be disabused of this notion. Life is now and the child is now. His concerns are now, the answers he seeks are for now questions, his feelings are now feelings. Respect him for the wholeness of himself at any given moment of his development. This is some of what I mean by Life Education. Not education *for* life, but education *through* life, through living it fully at any given moment.

Childhood is not a bridge to adulthood. Children live in childhood. You do not have to teach them to live. You do not have to teach them to feel life, to feel pleasure. I believe this happens in the womb, from the moment of conception on. The struggle to retain what is pleasurable and therefore life-oriented—what is therefore in the most basic sense of the term sexual—is the major focus of an alive yet unborn child.

Look then to the early years of childhood, to the joy and wonder apparent in a little child's discoveries about himself and the world he is part of. Children have a curiosity and a directness which comes from being open to all kinds of feelings.

The job of the educator: to help the child keep this openness, to help him stay open to his own feelings to start with and, as he grows, to the feelings of others, to support his desire to seek out what is pleasurable and what is positive in terms of his own growing sense of self—selfhood, if you will. Of this selfhood, sexuality is very much a part, if not the essential dynamic—the life-force—of child as well as man. Education is to nourish, to foster this life-force in the growing child. Education which urges him to forfeit it in exchange for greater conformity, greater tractability, wills children to be objects rather than people. Were this successful, we would, as D. H. Lawrence says, "see men die, then die ourselves."

The idea of teaching sex to children is a *reductio ad absurdum* of the whole concept of teaching subject matter rather than teaching human beings.

You do not have to "teach" sex to a child. Anyone who has ever had anything to do with small children knows they are very sensual people, forever drawn to those who are warm and loving, forever wanting to curl up with soft animals, forever turning to those experiences which expand rather than

diminish them, make them feel more rather than less joy in
being who they are. At least this is true of those children who
are allowed to grow without the stultifying effect of moral
attitudes imposed on them from without.

What, then, *is* sex education in a so-called free school like
Lewis-Wadhams?

First—rid people of the notion that Lewis-Wadhams is a
place where children play musical beds. The idea that in the
absence of moral or religious constraints children would be
fucking all the time suggests only that those who imagine this
are locked in the grip of a wish-dream of their own.

Sexuality has to do with feelings. Feelings have no morals.
They are neither good nor bad, right nor wrong. They yield
pleasure or they yield pain. It is best to stay in touch with
them, to be able to express them, to understand them, not to
be afraid of them. That is what we do here.

We have "sex seminars" each term. The children say what
they want to talk about. Paul and I, the participating adults,
introduce reading material. Sometimes films. Or to get things
going we sometimes begin by just talking about Words and
Images. Sexy words, warm words, nostalgic words, obscene
words, cozy words and words which make you feel lovely, or
sad or happy. People bring in pictures, magazine ads, posters,
record jackets, make collages. What is Sexy?

Sometimes the seminars work, sometimes they bomb.
There is no prescription for success. We sit in a circle, all of
us. Paul and I do not sit facing each other, as we've been
advised that when we do, we are likely to exchange meaningful glances and this gets everybody uptight. We accept this as
true, and it probably is true, everybody being a little uptight
to begin with. People come to this class because they want to
talk about themselves, the feelings they are troubled by, who

they are, if they are really anybody, if they are lovable, what will happen if they risk loving and what is "love" and what is "like." Not easy things to talk about. There are many silences. There is often a lot of laughter, which eases things up a bit. And there are tears, of course. We are close to one another, close enough to touch, to stroke, to hug. Given the chance to be themselves, most of these children are still sensual people, thank God, close to earth. Some stretch out full-length on the floor as tensions ease away.

We talk in this week's seminar about various inhibiting attitudes, about feelings like anger and jealousy and homosexual fears. People write about themselves, anonymously at first. I read aloud. People begin to reveal themselves as author. Smiles and nods and winks are exchanged. Later in the week people begin to read their own papers. I have been given permission to use at Goddard what they have written. Here is some of it:

> Love is something that happens right away when I see someone move or hear them speak. If I get a good feeling from a person when I first meet them, I know I can have something. If I notice someone and I'm not impressed, I could be friends with them but it wouldn't be special. I like to be safe too, so I begin to love someone who I can't really talk to, and I get unhappy.

> I would like to talk about anger and fear because sometimes I am afraid to show my anger and my fears. If I don't show my fear and anger, later I get very upset.

> I want to get fucked by Mick Jagger and then I want to fly away and forget about all the sex crap.

> I think boys become homosexual cause they feel they can't live up to the American super male image and maybe also they fear and mistrust girls and go to boys who have the same

feelings. These are my feelings and of course they make homosexuality seem the best and only way.

Fucking to me is something that I think about in like a dream or a fantasy. I am a virgin, so I would think it would be something big and fantastic, something that's way off in the distance and only happens in a dream, or in a fantasy . . . big green, blue, red and purple lights swirling in a dance hall, with people sweating and screaming, but my friend I talked to said it wasn't like that. It's quiet and soft, she said, like a field in summer or the river and the trees. I couldn't understand, she used such *strange* expressions!

Sexual Frustration As I See It

Sexual frustration is never being able to establish a boyfriend-girlfriend relationship with anyone. I should know, I'm an expert at being sexually frustrated. During the time I've been at this school I have been sexually frustrated in this way, four times. Sexual frustration is worrying about your masculinity or femininity as the case may be. If you are worried, you have a disadvantage because you then blame yourself for being frustrated, as in the first definition. I myself am unbelievably worried about my masculinity; but I try to keep it inside of me, because I don't want people to know it.

I'd like to just be with people more and do things like sledding and run inside and flop on the floor and Oh I love you I'm happy.

I'd like to talk about some of the things brought up yesterday. I'd rather talk than write. I don't know why I have a hard time writing. It's scary having the words still being there I think.

It seemed as if everyone yesterday was saying the same thing —that they were frustrated because they couldn't communicate to other people. And it seemed like when Herb read the papers, everyone felt close to everyone else, but then class was over and everyone went back to themselves.

I get angry cause I get scared and my face freezes in an ugly me. It exposes my ugly fear for all to see, and I wonder if expression around people I like. My face plays nasty tricks on anyone understands I don't really hate them, but that I'm just scared out of my wits. I daydream of being in bed with someone I love, or of trying to pick them up, and lots of times even this is ruined cause I get scared. I wish someone would come along and see through me. . . . It gets tiresome to have to keep fighting myself all the time. . . .

Last night I was angry because I felt inadequate. I felt like my body wasn't worth shit. I was angry. I am very angry at my mother. . . . I get jealous easily. A few people have told me that jealousy is a bad and useless quality to have, but I don't agree. . . . I am unsettled about homosexuality. . . . When I was young I got the impression that it was improper to touch *anyone* so I wanted to touch *everyone*. Homosexuality scares me so I try not to think about it. I do though.

I feel so alone. I want to love. I want to hold out my hand. I want to hug, I want to kiss. Sometimes I think I'm the only person who has the feeling I have. Who loves me when I love so many other people?

. . . I feel that too many people confuse making love with making out; I myself feel that. I won't try to define the difference, as I can't. As an example (a poor one but nonetheless an example) you can kiss a person without loving the person you kiss, yet kissing is an act of love. You should think about what I just wrote; as the only example I felt like writing.

I was with a boy last night and I was touching him and it really felt good. I was afraid but it did feel good, so now I'm just feeling good. Like walking slowly and looking around and feeling myself move.

ENTRY VIII

Thursday. Marti and Sam called a school meeting this morning to talk about bullying. No names were mentioned. No one was personally attacked. "Let's just talk about why people bully," Marti said, "not who they are or who did what to whom, for a change. We all know who they are anyway." General assent expressed.

Sam: I'd like to say that it's got so every place you go in this school this term there's someone letting his anger out on someone else. We could try to find out why they're so angry and help them express it in other ways.

Others: Being angry is being scared first. I used to be scared all the time but I didn't want to let on I was. Like, make a lot of noise and no one knows you're scared.

I don't see how it helps to hurt other people.

Well, if you think someone's always going to put you down, one way is you put them down first.

What Sam was saying about this term, I think a lot of us have given up on this term. I've about given up. It's like people can't get through to each other. There's always someone screaming around or crying. You feel like what can you do about it?

I try to detach myself.

You only get a lot of shit if you try to get involved, try to stop it or something.

I'd like to say [a solemn thirteen-year-old] I think the school is falling apart this term.

This meeting is getting disgusting. It's just everybody sitting around bitching again. I thought we were going to talk about how to help these guys stop their bullying?

Meetings don't generally help bullies get over their need to bully because bullies don't generally come to meetings, seeing in them simply another form of despised authority, another ruse of the "them" out to get "us."

Once Marti didn't come to meetings either. Now she does, and in fact often calls them. People call meetings for a variety of reasons, the ostensible one not always the prime mover. For little children and sometimes newcomers of any age there is a lot of exhilaration in the shouting of "ayes" and "nays," in waving hands and fighting for the floor, in being chairman and in the making and unmaking of countless rules—"sessions," as a recent visitor wrote me appreciatively, "where rights and powers are not determined by size and age, and where the air may be thick with 'fucks' but not with phoniness."

Marti, I think, has begun to see the meeting structure—and use it—as a way to extend the dimensions of her walled-in self. Wanting out of the self-constructed prison of her privacy, she still cannot altogether relinquish the safety she imagines lies in being at all times in control of situations and experiences and therefore herself.

Sam is another story. I am not sure what is happening to him this term, his second-to-last term in the school (he graduates in June). He has been copping out on classes, doesn't hang around with his old group of cronies, hasn't come to see me since the Christmas break. He has just stayed away, been absent from the life of the school—which seems to sum up my feeling about him these days. Yet here he is, teaming up with Marti, coming on strong with a pitch for school unity. Children continuously amaze me! This, if you let it happen to you, can be the yeast of teaching.

For whatever reasons, Sam and Marti's real concern for what is happening to the school made itself felt by others, including the gang of six terrorists no one names but everyone knows. All boys from twelve to seventeen. Only one, and that one not the ringleader, leaves. Jason, who is the ringleader, sits still for it. For a while. This in itself unusual. Others talk, and good feelings begin to take over:

I think bullying is making other people the scapegoat just so the scapegoat won't be you.

Why does there have to be a scapegoat?

Well, like a lot of us, maybe before they came here those guys who bully us got scapegoated somewhere else and think they would be here too.

If they don't think anyone cares about them . . .

How are you supposed to care about someone who's beating up on you all the time or threatening you?

Well, you can pretend to. Like you hang around and laugh when they beat up on someone else or make them cry or something. If you act like you're on their side, then you think it won't be you next time.

I just run when I see one coming. [A little kid.]

Laughter. Then indignation:

I don't see what's funny about it. To me it's sad. Sad for the bullies, I mean. People pretend to like them so they won't get hurt, or run and hide or keep very still and hope not to be noticed. I think that's sad. What if they knew we really wanted to like them? Wouldn't that help more?

Well, they are part of the community, after all.

I don't really *not* like them.

What we're really all trying to say, I think, is that we do care about them and they shouldn't think we only care about us. We really care about them too, and that's why we're having this meeting, to try to help, so wouldn't that help, just knowing that, I mean . . .

At this point Jason erupts:

If you want to know what would help me . . . I'd like to hit Herb, really hard. I'd like to hurt him. Then maybe I could stop bullying.

Chorus of "What for?" "What did Herb do to you?"

I knew what for. I had put Jason on trial term. After two years of trying to help him level off, I had finally told him before he went home for the holidays that he'd have to accept being on trial term when he came back and would have to leave at the end of winter term if he hadn't been able to level off by then. I knew that he could, if he chose, now focus on me as the villain instead of coming to grips with his own actions as the source of his troubles. I had to take that chance. Others were being hurt. I had to think about them too.

With this revelation, the others swung over to Jason's side.

Jason: If I can't stop bullying, I'm out. That's what the man says. OK, so I'm trying, but it's not fast enough for him. He's got to speed things up a little. If he thinks that's going to help . . .

There is not a child who has ever come here who does not feel that he has been hurt by an adult and who does not suffer from a sense of rage and perplexity because of what he feels has already happened to him and what he fears may happen to him again. One frightened little boy spent his first year here never speaking a single word to anyone over the age of seventeen. Under the armor of his truculence, Jason nurses the same wounds.

A surge of sympathy for him, outrage against me. I defend myself:

Jason is not bullying because I put him on trial term. I put him on trial term because of his bullying. Now he is trying to bully me. Well, I'm not going to be the scapegoat for you, Jason.

You say you have to stop bullying or else you're out, as though you had no other choice. You have another choice and you know it. Everyone is willing to help you, and yet you refuse help when it is offered to you, either by me or by other kids showing they support you. Now you say you can only level off if I drop the trial term.

The opposition says:

But he was leveling off.

I don't see how trial term is going to help anyway.

Pressure isn't going to help him. It'll only make it worse.

It's not fair, Herb.

What right have you got? . . .

I say:

It's not fair for others to get hurt. That is the reality of the situation and I think he needs to face it and come to terms with this reality.

I do have the authority to put him on trial term and I don't think the pressure he is feeling right now is necessarily a terrible thing for him.

The reality also is that he has not been leveling off. Why have so many of you come to me complaining about him? I think that ought to be faced by all of you too.

The opposition says:

We said we would try to help him, we were going to try. Why can't you give him a chance if we're willing to?

I say:

OK, I'd like to know how many of you feel he ought not to be on trial term. If the majority of you feel I ought to drop it, I'll drop it. Are you willing to say here and now that I should?

There is no answer to this question because at this point the proceedings are effectively disrupted by the school dog, Ruby, a mild-looking beagle-type animal everyone loves, going after a family cat who had strayed down the hill and is plainly considered by Ruby to be a poacher. When order is somewhat hilariously resumed, it is found that Jason has taken advantage of the uproar to slip quietly away.

Entry IX

I think about this. Meetings do not necessarily solve issues. They identify issues, rather, and the often complex current of feelings that goes along with them.

A "free" school generates its own clichés and can be subsequently haunted by them. New staff as well as new children are the most frequent victims.

Free love, for instance, does not necessarily mean boys always have to "want to" and girls always have to say "yes." Similarly, the right to vote does not mean one always has to vote. Both situations involve freedom of choice and what is meant by it. Freedom of choice adds up to something sensible only if one knows one's feelings in a given matter and is able to face up to the responsibility of what one chooses.

To recognize an impasse, an emotional dilemma, and to face up to the irrelevance of action under these circumstances is also freedom of choice. I think this is what happened this morning and why the meeting melted away.

I try to sort it out. The "way out" I offered proved unacceptable—to Jason, who simply absented himself when a showdown on his trial term appeared inevitable, and to the meeting itself, which took advantage of his absence to declare itself concluded, telling me quite plainly that below the surface of rage against me for my display of authority lay other, and contradictory, feelings. Perhaps they are reluctant to accept the responsibility for a "freed" Jason, reluctant to test their ability to help him, reluctant in spite of their anger against me to replace my authority with their own.

I think this is a dilemma children face often, an impasse they are caught up in again and again as they measure their strength against the demands of one or another situation and find themselves wanting. It is a feeling of inadequacy one must have enormous respect and compassion for. Who has not been there, or is not, to some extent, still there today? No one grows up, if ever, all at once. No one is always strong when he most wants to be. No one is always unfailingly certain he is equal to the task he sets himself or willing to risk failure to find out.

Children's sense of inadequacy—and it is partly an irrational fear of inborn limitation in those who have consistently been faulted for their failure to come up to someone's notion of success—is particularly poignant. They confront an external reality whose dimensions are still merely glimpsed, guessed at, whose vastness may be vastly overrated but whose power to hurt is not.

Still another question about this morning's meeting: Does the status quo the children in effect chose justify my putting Jason on trial term in the first place? I would like to believe it does, but I do not. It is one of the many times I—as authority —have felt dubious about the way I have exercised my prerogative, accuse myself of poor judgment and ask why.

Neill's experience at Summerhill with trial term led him to abandon it as a poor solution to the problems of the bully. If you cannot help the bully by reaching, getting through to him with a message he hears and responds to by letting go of his shield and his saber, you ought simply to ask him to leave. Trial term only puts his back up against you all the more, and with all the more reason. Why did I think—or hope—trial term would work for Jason?

It is simply that I like Jason and feel the depth of his hurt and do not want to tell him to pack up his belongings and go. I do not want to give up. Not yet.

ENTRY X

I stay up to listen to the late weather reports. Tomorrow, early morning, I leave for the Goddard weekend. Storm warnings, sub-freezing weather. Physical tensions everywhere in school. Attribute some of this to restraints imposed by the weather. I asked people if they thought it would help to write down what they were feeling about it.

It is so damn cold out that people don't usually go out. A lot of people stay in one certain building indefinitely because they don't feel like getting their socks wet or slipping on the ice.

Everyone becomes so bored that the only thing left to do is either bother other people, spit on the floor and ceilings and tables or just sleep.

In general, people just aren't feeling well. It seems like the best way to describe survival this term is each for his own. Sometimes I think things are hopeless but then I think about summer term when things are warm and I can move . . .

Sunday, 9 February—
Sunday, 16 February

Entry XI

The storm came, the snow piled up. I drove home from Vermont in early winter twilight tonight through the emptiness of winter landscape that a huge snow leaves behind it. Softness. An absence of people. Nothing moves across vast expanses of mountain whiteness; only the cars crawl along the Northway, and an occasional snowplow. A stop for coffee and reassurance that all human life has not departed this planet but congregates in warm, steamy places exchanging felicitations for survival.

Little flurries of snow continue to grace us most of Monday and Tuesday. The quiet ones tend to like it, I notice, and those who have formed fast friendships and take long snowy walks together and the little children who demand to be read to a lot and fall asleep early after a day of rushing in and out, boots on, boots off, long hair dried by the fire in the lounge and never enough food. It always seems to be snack time when the snows fall. And to fill in the empty spaces between there are meetings and more meetings. In some ways, the school seems in a state of siege.

New staff are perplexed by the undercurrents of tension and disaffection that keep people on edge a lot of the time and periodically break through the surface into shouting matches, the hurling of obscenities, insults, pushing, falling, tears. The bullies flourish, act as lightning rods, delightedly accumulate everyone's pent-up frustration.

Old staff reassure new staff that these things do not generally last and we discuss ways and means to absorb or deflect the shock waves that meanwhile buffet us.

A general school meeting follows staff discussion. No one wants to hear me when I suggest that the tensions do not necessarily mean that Lewis-Wadhams is falling apart but may instead mean that no one is getting enough physical exercise. All the same, after the bullshitting and bitching goes on for a good couple of hours, I say something like "Let's cut the talking and put on a record and dance." The effect is electric.

That was yesterday. Tonight, again the record player is on full force. People are dancing in the lounge, games are being played all through the house and the building is vibrating with noise and laughter. Thank God we have no near neighbors.

Entry XII

It is close to midnight. Jason came up the hill to see me about an hour ago. "Have you got a cigarette on you, Herb?" As good a ploy as any to justify that long, wet climb to my fireside. "Anything else?" "Well, yes . . ."

A pot of tea. Honey and lemon. Another cigarette. We talked, that is he did most of the talking, the words coming out in a rush with none of the usual silences and false starts and four-letter-word cop-outs. He talked about his future, his concern for what might happen to him, his love for his parents and how he felt about being a middle child. He talked about being lonely and feeling unwanted. Not directly, never saying in so many words that his hunger was for more than a couple of cigarettes and a cup of tea by the fire, but for affection and assurance he wouldn't be abandoned or hurt here as he has been elsewhere.

"I'll have a hard time looking at you tomorrow, Herb."

I hope he does not. He needs to cry. At what age are little boys induced obliquely if not directly to accept the myth of the unmanliness of tears? I hope he can look at me tomorrow and that someday he can cry.

Something of this I felt at Goddard last weekend: the inability of people to look at each other, touch each other, feel through to the very human meaning of what was being talked about, break through the surface noises that all the formally strung-out sets of words were making to the underneath of all of us. The last day, the last session, we did make a breakthrough of sorts. The last day ought to have been the first.

I did not say what I had come prepared to say, in terms, that is, of a prepared speech. Instead, I talked about what I thought had caused the uptightness that characterized most of the weekend, and how it was the same sort of uptightness that made communication between young people and adults so very difficult and often meaningless.

Children want answers and they want an honesty and directness that is very difficult for adults to give them. Adults, especially educators, get caught up in concepts and in a kind of verbalization of these concepts which conceals rather than reveals the humanness of what is being talked about. How many adults as children ever saw their parents naked? Ever saw them embrace or kiss each other? There still are many children today who have never seen their parents touch each other in a loving way.

I believe children must be witness to love: love free from guilt, from the sense of sin, from anxiety. If you look at it this way, all love is free. The notion of unfree love is an absurdity. What have the words "unfree" and "love" to do with each other?

In the early Goddard sessions the group—as a group—felt very much like young lovers to me. They were apprehensive, self-conscious, indecisive, afraid to begin—all elements of a first love affair. Only the love affair did not happen. Instead, the group polarized into two separate factions: those who saw sex education as a curriculum problem, and those who took the "humanist" approach.

I met a lot of nice people, of all ages, and once we were able to come together with the masks at least part way down, we also began to reach out and touch one another.

ENTRY XIII

Excerpts from tapes of Goddard discussion:

Herb: I think when a young person has difficulty or reservations talking to someone who on a psychological level he is very close to, then something has missed somewhere along the line. If a person can see an adult not as an educator, not as a teacher, but as a person, then something meaningful can begin to happen. And not always through words.

Someone last night talked about touching, holding, cuddling, feeling. These are all nonverbal ways of communicating. They are also sexual ways. Sexuality is not jumping into bed and fucking all the time. This is not what young people are into.

A young person last night said, "Wouldn't it be wonderful if I could feel close to somebody, lying next to somebody, feeling him?"

Last night a young person—who happened to state to all of us that he and his wife had lived together for a year before they decided to get married—told an older person that she was living in the past. The woman's response was very open. She became quite upset. I thought she was going to cry. She did not become threatened and she did not attack the younger person. She accepted the thought and she tried to work with it. Each was trying to feel what the other was feeling. They were trying to connect with one another and it didn't make any difference what were their ages. . . .

It is basically a feeling involvement. What is happening to individual people on a very feeling level and how can each of us support each other, help each other. . . .

Audience: I think we have to be very cautious about the ambiguity that's involved in feeling. . . . The preparation for adulthood doesn't mean that you have to do away with the now, but really the now takes on all that's meaningful in the sense that you are anticipating the future. What I'm concerned with is what do you mean by feeling? . . .

Herb: I think the personal struggles that each of us goes through are triggered by a wish for identity and pleasure. A sense of, Who am I? I think that one of the ways we will ever really know is to be able to cleanse our own souls, so to speak; to be able to let out those things which are inside. Someone who is terribly angry most of the time is someone blocked. Someone who is in physical tension all the time is blocked. . . .

Audience: Are you suggesting the release of all tensions?

Herb: I'm talking about the wish of man to become more

and more in touch with himself and to experience pleasure; to experience what it means to be a man or a woman, and not on an intellectual level alone; for an adult to be able to let out those childlike qualities which are within us all and which so many of us really try to keep down and not let out. This is my own personal struggle.

Audience: . . . What tensions are you going to release and what tensions are you going to inhibit, and some have to be. For example, you take some explorer who went to the North Pole. At the age of nine or ten he read about it and always wanted to go. Now what he had to do was put up a tremendous bout of self-discipline in order to gain the strength he needed . . . and as a result that tension wasn't something that was a distortion but was a positive contribution to his life because it spurred him on.

Herb: What tension?

Audience: What tension? The tension of not being able to do now what he wanted.

Herb: OK, this is the choice then that you as a single human being have to make. You will create tensions which in your terms become very positive tensions because in your terms what you want to do is make that dash to the Pole.

In the art world, if you want to be a great painter, you have to suffer like hell, and all the great painters seem to be those men and women who have suffered. So the two seem to go together, the great art and the suffering. I think this is a cultural myth which is now taken for the truth.

I think these are personal choices and not always on the conscious level. If you feel the necessity to suffer certain kinds of pain and tension in order to be that artist, that is your choice.

Audience: What is the criterion for choice? What is the

criterion for making priorities? I want to say that if it was the question of the Pole or a human being at stake, I think the human being would have to be picked over the inanimate Pole, but what is the criterion that each person should solve? Is it going to be completely arbitrary?

Herb: I can't speak for you.

Audience: Then we can't establish any community of meeting between us.

Herb: Why not?

Audience: If you can't speak for me and I can't speak for you, then there is no possibility of "we" speaking. You speak, I speak, and we never speak as "we."

Herb: In some sense this is true, but we are trying to reach out to each other right now.

[At this point the moderator attempts to close the discussion as irrelevant to the "topic," only to be met with the following statement by someone in the audience.]

Audience: We've been talking to each other and at each other all weekend about the need for relationships. We come to a discussion about it, we begin to get into it and we blow it again. Damn!

Herb: Well, then let's keep going.

ENTRY XIV

Money. A subject, like sex and freedom and all men are born equal, commonly labeled "Keep out of the reach of children." I think otherwise. Lewis-Wadhams has money problems as do most unendowed small private schools, and with the rising cost of living, they have become acute. Ends do not meet. We spend more than we make. Almost half of the children are here on some kind of tuition reduction, and I do not want to change that, nor do I want to raise tuition. Either course would mean not only that we would lose many of the children with us now, but also that we would attract henceforth only the children of the rich. That is not what we are all about.

I put the facts before a school meeting Thursday. If we want to keep our doors open without raising tuition, we have to find a way to cut down on spending. Food was the first thing we took a good hard look at. Orange juice every morning, seconds on milk, yoghurt twice a week, eggs every morning, bagels and cream cheese on Sunday, three snacks a day, butter and sour cream on baked potatoes, coffee at every meal for those over thirteen and so on. Allowances, school supplies and laundry, now included in tuition costs, were also talked about as possible money-saving areas.

It was a long meeting. Almost everyone there showed very real concern for the problem we face. With the exception of those few youngsters who regularly steal from the kitchen, romantically seeing themselves as outlaws, and the littlest ones, who figure the school goes on running no matter what or at least life goes on running so long as there is someone to take care of them, it was plain that between school and children, staff and administration, there is no dichotomy. We are one and the same. We are all of us Lewis-Wadhams.

Today, Saturday, one of the two committees formed to report back to the community on ways and means to cut food costs presented its findings. Two hours of discussion. Changes made. We wind up weary, but with a sense of accomplishment. All those many hours spent considering things precisely, like the proverbial cost of eggs, figuring, paring, substituting, adding, subtracting and dividing will yield us a savings of close to $2,000 a year.

If the second committee does as well on allowances, supplies and other miscellaneous costs, we can rest easy for another year.

Monday, 17 February—
Monday, 24 February

_____

ENTRY XV

What is government? Why government? Is it necessary? A necessary evil or a necessary good? What is democracy? Why democracy? Are we a democracy? Is America? Questions of this sort form a sort of leitmotiv in the life and times of Lewis-Wadhams. More accurately, perhaps a constant replay of theme and variations as the whole vast and complex subject of democracy in one or another of its aspects presents itself over and over again at Lewis-Wadhams. In a week I will talk about this at Auburn, invited to do so by a member of the psychology department. "Democracy and Children" is an amorphous and vaguely theoretical umbrella title for a subject I am passionately and personally concerned with. What to say of all the many things I can and want to say and think need to be said? Where to begin? I have thought about it a lot and continue to do so.

The question of "rights" exploded again here today, in a fashion by no means amorphous or even vaguely theoretical. Tocqueville, responding to his experience of early nineteenth-century American democracy, worried about the tyranny of the majority. I thought of that this morning when all hell broke loose in the Little Room, and again this afternoon when the community took an action which I consider to be an unwarranted assault upon the rights of the Little Room people.

It is a curious fact that although at least two of our seminars in government have come up with a workable constitution, bill of rights and amendment-making machinery for Lewis-Wadhams, neither has presented these to the community for ratification. Considered too binding if written down, or perhaps unnecessary. Written or not, constitutional safeguards are implicitly built into our day-to-day life. Which is not to say that the rights of one individual or another, one group or another, are not periodically treated as of no account. We come, then, to the matter of due process.

Today, Monday morning. The Little Room children find their barn home a shambles. Tables have been overturned, dress-up clothes are all over the place, blocks are strewn everywhere—the disarray is awesome. Once more, numbers had to accept a postponement.

It was a good hour before we got the place cleaned up, during which time tempers did not improve. The little children clearly had had it, and at the meeting we then held to determine what to do about the constant misuse the Little Room was being subjected to by older children it was unanimously decided to ban the rest of the community from the area except for classes. No exceptions. The announcement was made at morning snack time in the main lounge. Much ado from some of the older children, particularly three teen-age girls who like to play the Little Room piano. It is kept locked and in general is held in considerably more reverence than the piano in the lounge. Therefore it stays more or less in tune. The same cannot be said of the piano in the lounge.

Monday afternoon. A meeting is called by one of the three outraged girls who proposes that the piano be moved out of the Little Room. I was not present, but it was later reported to me that indignation at the Little Room children for daring to declare their premises out-of-bounds to others was widespread. Staff included. The notion was put forth that everything belongs to everybody and no one group has the right to deny any other group the use of school, i.e., communal, property. No one pointed out what to me appears to be at the heart of the matter: Majority feelings do not justify the stampeding of minority rights. So the piano was promptly voted out of the Little Room, to the consternation of the Little Room children who, quite rightly, consider their piano an integral part of their program. Furthermore, no one pointed out that the Little Room children had always been willing to share what was theirs, never withholding permission from anyone else to use the Little Room until it became clear that what was going on in their absence was not so much use as abuse.

If the majority have the right to vote the piano out of the Little Room, have they not also the right to vote out whatever else they choose—including the Little Room children? How abandoned they must have felt this afternoon with no one to speak up in their behalf. I have strong feelings about the little children. They need all the support we can give them. They do not need desertion. Desertion is what they got this afternoon. I am sometimes exasperated with staff. This is one of those times. A theoretical position in favor of a communal ideal ought not to blind one to the hurt that may be inflicted on the weak by the strong.

Entry XVI

One can always count on Sandy. Although he had taken little part in the Little Room crisis yesterday, true to form he mulled it over quietly in his own mind, and today, after lunch, called a meeting. Speaking out in support of his Little Room colleagues, he said they were not willing to accept the proposal passed yesterday. "We want the piano to stay in the Little Room. You have no right to move it out. It belongs to us."

Cries of "It belongs to everybody!"

"No," I said, "it belongs to the little kids."

A debate ensues.

I say: The piano, as much as the blocks, the paints and the easels, the fish tank, the swings, the Jungle Jim and the sink and the ragdolls and the costumes and all the little chairs and tables and cushions and the rest of it, belongs in the Little Room. It is as much a part of the physical structure of the Little Room as the Little Room itself is part of the academic structure built around the needs of the little children. The only people who have a right to vote the piano out of the Little Room are the Little Room people themselves.

Tim: If the majority feels . . .

We fought it out an hour or more before we could arrive at an understanding about those areas of Lewis-Wadhams life subject to majority vote or community decision, and those areas which hopefully reflect community feelings but in the last analysis are a matter of built-in constitutional rights which evolve out of feelings for one another.

It was also pointed out that whereas the piano in the Little Room is essentially part of the academic program for the younger children, the piano in the lounge is not part of any-one's academic program. Why not vote it out of the lounge, where it takes an indiscriminate beating from anyone who feels like banging it, and move it to the art room?

"This much inconvenience up with which they will not put," muttered a staff member.

No reply.

The meeting adjourned. The piano stays in Little Room.

The rest of the afternoon I devote to my Auburn speech—"Democracy and Children." The process of self-government here is in a constant state of flux. Could it be otherwise when the aim is to achieve democracy on a personal as well as on a social level?

I think this is what democracy meant at one time in America and what is missing from it today. A number of people, particularly the young, no longer believe their personal wishes for self-fulfillment can be realized through democracy as it manifests itself in the American technological culture. When we were more agrarian and pastoral, and horizontally rather than vertically spaced out, perhaps closer to our roots, we were able to express more directly, on a personal level, the thoughts, ideas and feelings which moved us. Perhaps we believed or even knew that people (social) were listening and that you and I (personal) did not have to shout to be heard, or decide, as many have today, that it is not even worthwhile shouting, for we are not ever going to be heard anyway.

There must have been a time when America did stand for individual liberty and freedom, which I translate on the unconscious level to mean personal gratification of ego and body. Today individual liberty as individual effort no longer makes sense. It is the team, the conglomerate, the institution, the system, that is all-powerful. Impersonal, even anonymous, no longer having anything to do with what you or I or the person next door wants.

Entry XVII

The "man" put in an appearance today—an inspector

from the New York State Department of Education, Fire Division. People are always asking me whether "free school" children don't have trouble in their dealings with the so-called outside world. I was able to observe no such trauma in today's contact. On the contrary, the inspector, an amiable as well as a skilled professional man, played Pied Piper to a number of children who took the tour along with the two of us and listened intently to what was being said. Lewis-Wadhams is highly fire-conscious, perhaps because of the episode with the Northway dynamite sticks, perhaps because we have all had occasion up here to see what fire can do—and has done—to others in our neck of the woods. Neighbors are few and far between, fire hydrants not part of a rural country landscape, and fire rules are seen to make sense, life-and-death sense, to all but a few intransigent holdouts against any rules "the man" makes. At any rate, it was smooth going this morning. The inspector was pleased, the fire chief was pleased, and so were we.

Entry XVIII

The rights of children have until recently been almost totally ignored or, worse still, considered nonexistent, in this (self-styled) democratic society of ours. Further notes on the Auburn talk.

Item: Children's rights beginning to enter arena of judiciary. Various cases brought before high courts reflect protest against exclusion of children from guarantees of First Amendment.

Joshua Mamis, defending his right to circulate a petition for the ouster of his school principal: ". . . there is something wrong with a school system which teaches the principles of the Bill of Rights but then doesn't allow me to put these principles into action. . . ."

Fortas majority opinion of Supreme Court affirming right of grade school children to engage in symbolic protest: "In our system, state operated schools may not be enclaves of totalitarianism. School officials do not possess absolute authority over their students. Students in school as well as out of school are persons under the Constitution."

Until now, schools have simply ignored the Bill of Rights (as have parents) in the name of discipline. Hallowed discipline, discipline that relegates liberty and freedom to the back of the bus.

Item: Discipline. The notion that children must be disciplined, i.e., cajoled, threatened, bribed, punished from without, implies lack of trust in young people. Also lack of trust in democratic process, inability to accept dissent as crucial to our health as a nation, a people, persons—children included.

Discipline as an expansive not a repressive force. Inner discipline construed—misconstrued—as permissiveness. Why? Most people never achieve it?

Item: The "democratic way of life" is the "American way of life." No one thinks of this as permissive—unstructured or undisciplined. A "free country" means liberty, equality, human dignity, the constitution, cherry trees. It means self-government, due process, freedom of choice, a say over one's own life and how one wants to live it.

Exception: the under-eighteeners. Connotations of freedom as applied to a school like Lewis-Wadhams—a euphemistic way of saying children can raise hell here and get away with it.

Item: Children are concerned with the same things we are—self-esteem, identity, warmth, love, security. Children are born with a sense of belonging to the human race. Why disinherit them? Why separate childhood qualitatively from manhood?

Item: Why separate children from childhood? Childhood is a time to grow in, to learn in. Is there a better way for children to "learn" democracy than to "live" it? Living it, they continuously evaluate and test its tenets. They meet head-on the conflict inherent in its concept (Tocqueville again?), the conflict between the "I" and the "we," individual self-interest and community self-interest, resolved now one way, now another.

Trial and error as a part of growth. Children want to arrive at their own conclusions, need time, tolerance, patience and awareness on part of supporting adults that mistakes will be made.

Item: To children who live the democratic experience, liberty, equality, freedom of choice and the rest of the rhetoric commonly on the tongues if not in the hearts of most Americans cease to be abstract concepts. They become part and parcel of a child's sense of self and of self-worth, natural extensions of his wish to live life fully and to grant others the same right and privilege.

Of Lewis-Wadhams in a semiperpetual state of flux, I record one of the most complete turnarounds I can remember. The school voted a few days ago to make Jason pro tem director until the end of term, if I would step down. I said of course I would. If it was a put-on—after all, I had placed him on trial term—I answered in the same vein, adding that I would be glad to do what was asked of me in the interest of school unity. Laughter. But, as a matter of fact, I don't think it a bad idea.

End of a long week. A little better than three weeks to go before end of term. I too look forward to spring.

Thursday, 27 February—
Tuesday, 11 March

Entry XIX

The usual end-of-term jitters afflict everybody. A cold afflicts me, keeps me house-bound for a week. I emerge from hibernation to attend an "open house" to which I have been invited beginning at 11:00 P.M. Bedtimes are an issue once more—the little children are up until all hours, the bullies, including Jason, continue to raise hell, the staff absorb a lot of punishment and in general it is a repeat of the last week or so before the winter holiday.

The next morning I am presented with a petition signed by twenty-one children who say they want permission to leave before the end of the term.

This evening, during discussion period, I say that I have thought about this all day and have come to the conclusion that those people who want to leave should do so with no questions asked, no more talking about why they want to leave or what we can do to make them change their minds or even what can be done to make people feel better about this last week or so of the term.

"Maybe if those who feel that way do leave, the rest of us who want to stay out the last week can do so peacefully, without having to listen to the constant bitching.

"No one *has* to be here. It's your right to withdraw if you want not to be here. The choice is yours. You make it."

A captured look on some people's faces. A general air of martyrdom. Sighs and groans.

ENTRY XX

The unsettling and discouraging thing about my talk at Auburn was that no one asked any but superficial questions. It was my first up-close brush with what politicos call the "hard-working, conscientious, nonrevolutionary, well-mannered, thinking college students who make up the majority of the college class." I prefer the minority. This comes to mind now because of the response I got—or rather, did not get —when I told them that ten days or so ago by majority vote of the school I was no longer director but had yielded my place to Jason. Yes, they laughed. That was all. No one asked why. Why Jason wanted to be director, why the school voted to let him be, why I agreed or what would happen next. No one, in fact, asked me any questions about anything during the meeting. Later there was some "informal" talk. Here again, for the most part I found a blandness, a submissiveness. No one emerged, no face or voice or look, from courteous— to be sure—but deadening anonymity.

Deadening and deadened, at least on the surface, this faceless majority. Who knows what feelings lie buried beneath the passivity?

Here today, all the tumult and shouting and the bursting

into tears and the hangdog looks and phony cynicism of the last few weeks came to an abrupt and dramatic end. The community, perhaps gaining the support they needed from what I said at last night's discussion, voted out the four bullies —Jason, Tim, Donald and Steve—for the rest of the term.

All is quiet now. The four are housed for the night in a local motel, pending arrangements to be made with their parents to fetch them or otherwise arrange for their various trips home.

Saturday, 15 March—
Tuesday, 18 March

Entry XXI

A quiet weekend. No meetings. In and out of the Main House on a windless Saturday, I hear the record player going in the lounge. Staff are reading to children of assorted ages. Upstairs Vina is giving hair washes. Someone is making cookies. The smell is warm and sweet coming from the kitchen. I stand with Clyde in the doorway and we talk about the pros and cons of getting a new truck, putting in a larger vegetable garden this spring, someday maybe raising beef stock, and that it is about time for the annual turnover of old hens for new. No one wants to eat the old chickens. This year there will be seventy-five of them. Clyde silently, stealthily I would almost say, attends to their demise and distribution to friends and family. A lot of sentiment gets attached to the things that grow around here, the animals that is. Including our two frowsy old sheep; you'd think nobody would care very much about them one way or another.

Entry XXII

Monday morning opens with a grand "war game" played between the Little Room children and the Middle Dome ones. Artillery is passed out in the form of Little Room blocks and ground rules are laid. Anyone killed must stay dead for fifty seconds before being reborn to fight again. You laugh and run and fall down, wait the near-minute out, get up and run, shout, scream, laugh and fall down again. No one gets hurt. No one wins. No one loses. It is not really a matter of "life and death." It is a game.

A truce is declared with the arrival of morning snack time. Hot chocolate and crackers. Austerity regime: cookies are only for Saturday nights and for parties, now.

I find this on my desk in the afternoon, from Donna, in her familiar roundish hand:

> Someone came up to me and said "I love you." I said "I love you, too," and walked away very puzzled at what she said. Love, what does that mean? I asked myself what does it mean and how do you show it to someone, how? I was very upset for the rest of the day and then Herb came up to me and asked "What's the matter?" and I said "Nothing," but that one word, *love*, was really bothering me. He said, "OK, but I think something is really bothering you, but if you don't want to tell me, then OK, but I love you" and he left.
>
> That word, there it was again, love, why does everybody say "I love you" to me, why? I went into my room and put on my fur coat and went outside. It was a beautiful snowy day out and I decided to go for a walk. Just as I was about to start walking, Cara came up over to me and asked if she could go with me. I said yes, so we started to walk down the street, the snow flakes falling on our noses and eye lashes. I felt so stupid over a stupid word like love, it was such a beautiful day, how could anybody be so stupidly unhappy.

After we had walked a ways Cara asked me why I was so unhappy and I said nothing, but she said there was something that was making me upset. Then I let it out and I said to her, "You see, today someone came up to me and said 'I love you,' and I didn't know what it meant" and Cara said, "What, the word love?" I nodded and she said to me, "Yes, sometimes I don't know what it means. It's a word with no true meaning, it's what you want it to mean just like the word 'hate,' there's no true meaning to that word either." "Aren't they two opposite words?" I asked. "Yes, if you want them to be," she said.

We went on talking for a long time and didn't realize how far we went and how dark it was getting and all of a sudden Cara stopped and said "Hey, we better turn back because it's getting dark and it's almost time for supper." So we turned back for school. When we got back, we saw Herb again and he came up to me and said, "You sure look happier now." I said, "I feel better, too, because I found out the true meaning of the word and I'll tell you after supper when I talk to you." He said OK and he asked Cara and I if we wanted service and we said yes. In a few moments he came back out with our suppers and we sat down to a good meal.

After supper I would tell Herb about the word love! After supper Herb came up to me and asked, "Do you want to talk now because I have time?" I said yes and kissed Cara good-bye and went down to the office with my arms around Herb and as we walked down I thought, "Right now I know the true meaning of the word love and Cara was right, it's what you want it to mean and it's there when you want it to be there and that's a very special way to feel."

THE END

DONNA

INTERIM

ENTRY I

Golda Meir once said, "The war will be over when Nasser loves his children more than he hates Israelis." I think there is a profound truth in this. Look at our own country, our own attitudes toward youth. A youth cult, yes. Women long past their fifties call each other *girls*. Men with thinning hair and paunches play poker weekly with the *boys*. But what of those who really are young, the boys and girls in their teens, the young men and women in their twenties? Do we love them? I wonder. No, I do not even wonder. I don't honestly think we do. I think we fear them.

Vide our attitudes toward the "unrest" on campus. We say the divine duty of educators is to teach young people to think. We ask them to think, to question, to create alternatives to the problems facing us as a nation and as a world community. When they come up with alternatives which expose the falseness of our way of life, the dichotomy between what we say we are all about and what we actually are all about, we develop a kind of selective deafness. We don't want to hear this.

We talk about the need for rational discourse but do not engage in same, the need for tolerance but show none ourselves, the right to dissent but punish this in a variety of ways, some subtle, some not so subtle. The ultimate penalty for outspoken dissent, of young or old—for that matter, of black or white, Spock, Coffin, Cleaver, Lee Otis Johnson, Philip and Daniel Berrigan, Newton, etc., etc.—is jail, political suicide or, finally, an expatriate existence.

A new weapon. There is talk now of the Federal Government cutting off financial aid to those students who cause campus unrest or a disruption of the status quo. When federal, state and local authorities invoke the law to curtail or eliminate political activity on campuses throughout the country, is it any wonder there is little respect for authority? Or for a political system so misunderstood and misapplied that it seeks to perpetuate itself as a bulwark against change rather than responding to the living, changing needs of a living, changing society? Are not students merely articulating these needs, as did Madison, Jefferson and Adams a couple of hundred years ago? Who remembers, by the way, that they were by no means old men, these framers of our Constitution?

Entry II

A week of our three-week spring holiday has already slipped by. There is little in the still wintry landscape to suggest the season's change. Here and there a little clump of early, spiny green leaves appears above the snow, a brief blossom borne for a fragrant day or so, causing great delight and confusion to Sigrid, who does not understand you cannot pick up a flower and put it down again as you would a toy or a book or a furry panda bear. Mystery of growing things.

The dog goes ape over a thawed patch of brown earth, barks and barks, dislodges a wet, cold, muddy stone, digs and digs. Cats put tentative paws out, retreat to warmth of perch over kitchen oven. Are the days growing longer, the sun warmer? The willows down by the river show the palest of color. One can hear the sounds of water under the ice.

Reading Norman Mailer: *Armies of the Night.* I'm impressed with his sincerity, tired of his bad jokes, envious of his power to use words. His rhythm is infectious. His vitality. He stays with me. He is one of the saner ones. In a schizoid world, where is sanity, where is reality? We are manipulated by game-players.

"They are our leaders," writes A. S. Neill. "Yet pathetic as a man who has fears of walking down a dark street. How can men who are so basically anti-life not destroy it eventually?"

They are sick and psychologically pathetic, Neill says, but how difficult it is to feel compassion for them. What possible dialogue on a reality level can one have with men who speak in double-talk of antipersonnel weapons, protective reaction strikes, body counts—a vocabulary invented to camouflage the fact that men are dying.

I'm worried about my kids. I'm worried about the people I know and love. I'm jolted by how far out *we* must seem to the others. There is a fullness within me right now. I want to reach out, to touch the people who can effect change, can bring safety and security to this world, so that my children, anyone's children, can grow with the knowledge that although we have the power to destroy heretofore vested only in the wrath of God, we will never use it because life is precious.

Life *is* precious. We are a very small place in a very large world. I hope we have the time.

Crazy, lovely, chaotic Norman Mailer, gutsy Norman Mailer, attempting to resurrect a dying, if not already dead, city from the ashes of indecision, compromise and despair. I don't know you, Norman Mailer, but I like what you say. You let your humanism show, your humanness, and I like you for that. It is uncommon.

Entry III

Inevitable this time of year a flood of parental inquiries about how their children are doing at Lewis-Wadhams. What they mean by "doing" and what I mean by it are often two different things. Apples and pears. I try to help parents see what is happening to children here the way I see it and the way they—the children themselves—feel it.

It is not easy for parents who experience a child's growing sense of independence as a rejection of themselves to feel other than hurt and confused. It is not easy for a parent who is certain that he loves his child to see that trust is a part of love. It is not easy for a parent to understand that if a child seems to have unlearned some of what he supposedly "knew" when he came here, he is only making room in himself for a new kind of learning to take hold, in time.

If a parent asks his child what he is learning at school, he is likely to get a dour look, a shrug of the shoulders or, even worse from a parent's point of view, an "I dunno." If he asks his child whether he goes to classes, he is likely to get an equivocal "Sometimes." Or an unequivocal "Don't bug me." Or, with angelic innocence, "What classes?"

Translate: Questions and Expectations (Parents)
Into: Pressures and Demands (Children)

From the mailbox—Stewart's mother:

From conversations with Stewart you obviously do not have him going to classes and it doesn't sound like they began until just recently. I think you should carry out the agreement that Stewart go to classes (if they exist) . . . will come home unable to deal with others. . . .

C. L.

From Sara's father:

". . . first two years an outstanding success. . . . I note that one of the by-products of a free atmosphere is the development of considerable curiosity in Sara . . . various questions asked . . . subjects in which interested.

Other side of coin . . . whether achieving mastery of fundamental subjects with which most adults . . . conversant.

I note Sara is now 15 years old . . . now entering what would ordinarily be first year of high school . . . tells me has had no English and no mathematics. . . .

To C. L.:

Yes, classes do exist and No, I don't *have* anybody going to them. They go because they want to go. Stewart, who is called Stuey here, does not want to go. Not yet. He is 13 and is busy playing Little Caesar and throwing his weight around. He is enjoying it that way. So are his friends. They are a gang of hoods. For now Stuey is a hood, too.

To Sara's father:

Sara went too far, too fast, too soon, taking in great gulps of intellectual material before she got here. She knows it, you know it, I know it. We have all talked about it together and separately. She has called a halt, to the surface commotion anyway. She wants to catch up with herself, her inside self. We do not teach English as a separate course or class here, but use it—reading, writing, organizing of one's thoughts and ideas—in all our classes. Sara does a lot of reading and writes —mostly for herself and her friends—stories, poems and letters. She speaks eloquently when she is moved to do so and is listened to. She despairs at the thought of numbers but knows what you expect of her. We have talked about this too. I am glad you are patient and feel good about the school and about Sara in it. She is a lovely girl. She is just 15.

Time. There it is again. Mostly I plead for time. Is the notion of time so abstract as to be meaningless, or so altered by the swiftness of life today that it has come to mean something one lacks rather than something one has been given, a natural gift of life?

I see time as a gift of great beauty and of great value in a child's life. Yet children are always being rushed. They are being rushed into learning, they are being rushed into achieving, they are being rushed into making decisions, they are being rushed into growing up. Into *being grown-up* rather as though being grown-up were a kind of reward to be earned for having endured childhood.

(A memory. A couple of years ago a mother and son came for an interview. The mother, very charged up, talked a lot, was concerned about many things. An hour or so went by. I asked the boy—William was his name—if he had any questions he wanted to ask me about the school. "Yes," he said, "do they have any rest periods here?" I said he could rest all day here if he felt like it. I don't think he quite believed this, but his mother did. No William at Lewis-Wadhams.)

Times change and time changes. It gets telescoped. The faster we move, the less time we seem to have. And the more pressure. I wonder if the pressures of our hurry-up-and-get-there society do not in turn build new pressures, contributing to man's feeling that he no longer controls his existence and is out of touch, human, personal, animal touch, with the forces that do.

Laura Ingalls Wilder is as often and as avidly read here as *One Flew Over the Cuckoo's Nest, Catch-22* and Hesse. The long journey halfway across the continent in a covered wagon delights children. Space is felt, distance, the earth. Hazards one can feel and touch are experienced, and the passage of time.

I am not suggesting a return to a pastoral yesterday. I am suggesting that some of the pressures parents bring to bear on children reflect the growing constriction of their own lives, reflect their own anxiousness, their sense of something missing that has to be made up for—somehow.

So I am always pleading for time, and for trust. A child really may know what is good for him. He knows when he is hungry, tired, needs to yawn, stretch, jump, climb, laugh, cry, go to the bathroom, shout. A child knows a lot about himself and his needs. Support him and trust him, I want to say to parents, and to teachers too. A lot of the time this is really the only answer which makes any sense. Unfortunately, a lot of the time this is not understood or is not acceptable. It does not relieve the pressures and anxieties the parent feels—the parent, not the child.

Witness: A boy we lost after only a year here. He came last fall, a gray-faced, awkward, silent little boy of twelve. A thin, crushed little person. He had a brilliant older sister. Everyone in his family had degrees and honors. It was not this way with Danny. His reading was minimal, so was his speaking. There was talk about a learning block, a learning disability; in technical terms he was described as a dyslexic. His parents, professional people, thought a looser environment might help.

All his first fall term here, Danny hung around doing not much of anything. He was quiet, a nonparticipant. He'd lean against a wall during meetings, never raise a hand, never say anything. He never got in anyone's way.

In December the snows came and Danny discovered sledding. All day, every day, in all kinds of weather, Danny sledded. He and Sam Johnson (age twelve) made friends, and the two of them went sledding day in and day out.

His mother writes:

> The weekly telephone calls throw us into a state of gloom again. He says that class now takes place but that he doesn't go very often. What does he do aside from sledding? With whom does he spend his time? I have visions of him moving about like a lonely shadow amidst boisterous activity. . . .

I answer:

> For whatever the reasons, this is the impression he wishes you to have. I believe it may come out of his reluctance to tell you that he is not only not going to classes but that he enjoys it this way.

He and Sam had discovered a common interest in photography and began coming to classes regularly and working in the darkroom. He came to discussions and to meetings and began to talk. He began to fill out, his face had color, he looked happy.

I wrote:

> Right at this moment it is snowing and he and Sam Johnson have come into the Staff House to warm themselves. They are both covered with snow and their faces are beautiful. They are now in the process of cutting a cake which Danny made. I should say a lemon custard pie, which from what I hear, will be divided up among five people. . . .

Spring came. A group of the middle kids, eleven to thirteen, came to us saying they wanted a theatre workshop, a week's seminar. They wanted to do *Winnie-the-Pooh*. Danny came to the first meeting. He wanted to play Winnie. He read the part straight off. He memorized it. We put it on. Danny played Winnie. No, he had not yet "gone to classes." In the fall, I thought, he might begin to. Come and go, at least. Try it.

August:

Dear Herb:

This is to let you know that Danny will not be returning to Lewis-Wadhams next term. While we agree with you that he benefited greatly from the year with you, we feel that another decision will be better for him at this time.

Our unanimous decision is X School. It is highly structured—therapeutically oriented—outstanding ability to provide individualized needs. They considered it remarkable that Danny has made substantial gains in reading in spite of no formal instruction. However, he is still behind where he should be. . . .

. . . hopeful a year or two will suffice to get him home where we *really* want him to be anyway.

One more from the mailbox, the last for today: ·

Both —— and I have been up to the school to visit in the past two weeks and we both felt that the boys seemed happy and at ease in their surroundings and with the other people, and this is fine. However, we are both rather disturbed about what I might call the anti-intellectual feeling which seems to pervade the school.

I'm not suggesting the formal, highly structured environment of the public school but more the guidance and motivation required to develop in young children the skills needed to pursue and develop . . . learning potential. . . .

E. W.

To E. W.:

I understand your concerns, they are also ours. What do you mean by intellectual? I would have to know that before I can comment on why you should find us anti-intellectual. I do not

think we are. I do not think we are anti-anything which lights
up a child's face, his spirit, his whole person. Stars, sky, a
book, a brook, a flute, counting, building a kite, flying it,
making a tower of blocks, knocking it down, any number of
things and ways people learn. You cannot always *see* learning,
E. W., in fact, rarely. Or know where it is coming from and
what is happening inside a child to allow his hunger for it to
surface and become visible.

What *is* learning? We are beginning to talk about this
more and more. With six years of voluntary classroom
experience behind us, we have practice as well as theory to
draw on. We ask not only, what is learning, but also, when
does the desire to learn become tangible or visible, or, when
one senses that it wants to be made tangible and visible, *expe-
riential* in short, what does one do about it?

When a child comes into a classroom voluntarily I—the
teacher—must assume there is something he wants. He does
not have to be there. He is there because there is something
he wants to experience. He may have no idea consciously
what it is. I think it is part of a teacher's job to help create an
environment where a child is going to be able to make conscious those unconscious feelings, at whatever level or degree
he or she is able to.

I think skills follow the experience, which is preceded by
the desire to know on an internal level. A child enjoys being
read to and at some point he wants to learn how to read. The
passive attitude gives way to the positive aggressive attitude.
The best a teacher can do is help him decode all those letters
and sounds as rapidly as possible. He wants to experience
reading for reasons known or unknown to himself. The reasons do not matter and motivation does not enter into it. You
do not have to motivate him. He wouldn't be there in the first
place. The child here comes out of his freedom, the freedom
which has allowed something to surface. He comes and brings
a wish, a desire, a gift to you in the classroom.

I once did a writing seminar with the older children. It

was just writing. Putting something down on paper. What they wanted to do and felt they needed to do most was to get over a real fear of putting something down on paper. A very real block was present. So my technique was to build it up slowly. We weren't interested in style.

I asked them a question and they answered it in one written word. Then another question to answer in two words, and so on, very simply building, so that by the end of the week they were writing. I was not concerned with getting across an unconnected notion of what spelling was, or grammar or even content. I wanted to help them get down to the physical experience of writing, the emotional experience of committing words to paper.

This means, for the most part, an active role for the teacher. A nonjudgmental role. It is part of a teacher's responsibility to help a child feel out what is inside him. It may be reading. It may be writing. It may be working in the science lab. Or playing the cello. Or listening. Or watching, or sewing or singing.

Whatever it be, it means listening to and seeing children with your whole being and not just with your brain.

It requires skills, enthusiasm, dignity. Teaching is a creative act.

Kate Snitzer (staff meeting on
new academic program)

Entry IV

Mika wonders what it would be like to spend the summer in a foreign country. No, not a tour, just to live somewhere for a while. Somewhere different.

Kate thinks it is a lovely idea and probably would appeal to other teen-agers here. But why summer? Why not winter?

Mika: Right, anything to get away from winter. Where? Everyone would want to go.

Herb: Well, not everyone. Everyone would be nice, but . . .

Mika: All right, where, Herb? Say six or eight of us.

Kate: Where it's warm.

Mika: And not too different. If a bunch of us are going, we'd have to speak some English or we'd really be lost.

Herb: Would you want to be with some staff?

Mika: Of course, Herb. Let's take Paul. What about Israel? We could live on a kibbutz. Next January, Herb, for the winter term. What do you say?

Today:

> April 16, 1969
> Israel Government Tourist Office

Dear Mr. Snitzer:

Thank you for your letter of April 2nd, advising us of your plans to send a group of students to live in Israel early next year. . . .

Entry V

The staff has been back for the last two days, and is now in the midst of preschool workshops. Dave Hartman came to see me in my office this afternoon to tell me he is leaving. I know this has been in the back of his mind for some time. There is a time when a person has to move on, he says. He has been here almost four years! For now, for him, I know he is doing what he has to, what he wants to. It is hard for him to talk about it. He has friends here.

A parent just rang me to ask if his boy should bring a fishing rod with him. I must remember to ask Clyde when the fishing season begins. The snow has begun to melt in earnest now, large brown patches of earth spreading across the splotchy white meadows, pines dripping, eaves dripping, birds returning.

SPRING

ENTRY I

On my desk the following:

BOOK OF SEASONS

> SPRING IS
> FLOWERS AND
> BIRDS

> SUMMER IS
> ICE CREAM

> FALL IS COLORED
>   LEAVES

> INDIAN
> SUMMER IS
> INDIANS

> WINTER IS
> SKIS

Laura is eight. Her crayoned illustrations are vivid. Her observations are accurate. Yes, Laura, spring is flowers and birds. It is also people, animals, bicycles, fishing rods, hiking boots, sleeping bags, grass greening, twilight lengthening . . . everyone out, doors clattering, spring rain.

ENTRY II

A week has gone by. I don't know where. Last night Mika called from down the hill. She and Craig wanted to talk something over with us.

The evenings are still cool. The sun's warmth in the North Country is really illusory until mid-May or even later. In spite of soft evening skies and birds nesting in new-green branches of the birches and elms, we keep a fire going against the night's chill.

Craig looks more fragile than ever, intent, apparently, upon studying the embers in the fireplace, the glass of wine in his hand, anything but the faces of Kate and myself, and now of Mika, who comes in from the kitchen with a mug of hot cocoa and settles herself comfortably on the floor across from him, leaning back against Kate's chair, and also looking at no one. The conversation goes something like this:

Herb: Well, who's going to start?

[A long silence. Mika, under her long eyelashes, takes a stealthy look at Craig. He seems impervious to all but the fire. He continually shifts his position.]

Kate: Herb, why don't you start? You have a pretty good idea why Mika wanted to come up here and have a meeting with us.

Herb: Okay. From what I understand, Mika feels that

Craig is making unfair demands on her and she is upset about it. Is that about right?

[Both nod agreement.]

Herb: Can you take it from there, Mika?

[I know it is hard for her. I know Mika does not like to demand anything for herself. It is hard for her to. She is unusually sensitive to others' needs. Now she is, at thirteen, becoming aware of her own. It is still a struggle to say so. Yet that's why she is here tonight.]

Mika: Well, what bothers me is that Craig really gets upset if I look at another boy or if I walk holding hands with someone else. He gets angry. I think he really gets jealous but he won't say anything. He just mopes around and then *I* get upset. I don't think this is good for me *or* him.

Craig: It's not really anger. I don't really get angry. I get upset and jealous. I don't know what to do about it. I don't really like it when Mika's with someone else.

Herb: What do you think will happen if she's with someone else?

Craig: I don't know. That's what upsets me. I get scared.

Kate: Are you saying, Craig, you feel more frightened than angry?

Craig: I really don't know, Kate. All I know is I get upset, as though Mika just doesn't care for me anymore, as though she might just go off with someone else.

Herb: Does Mika know that's how you feel?

Craig: I've tried to tell her. I think she understands.

Mika: I do understand. But it doesn't change how I feel.

Craig: I know that, Mika. Like, I understand you too, Mika. I really try to.

Mika: I don't feel good knowing that every time I'm with

someone else, I'm being watched. Craig is always watching me.

Herb: You said a minute ago, Craig, that it upsets you to think Mika might go off with someone else, that it scared you to think that might happen. If it did happen, what would it do to you, Craig. Have you thought about that?

Craig: Yes, I've thought about it a lot, Herb. It would hurt like hell. I'd feel lousy, Herb. That's all.

Herb: I know you'd feel like hell, Craig, but I don't think that's all. I think there's more to it than that.

Craig: You mean . . .

Herb: How would you feel, Craig, losing Mika? How would you feel about you, I mean.

Craig: I'd feel like a failure. I'd think I was a failure, Herb. A loser again.

Herb: Well, if you really want the relationship with Mika and really value her, how is it that your actions seem to have the opposite effect?

Craig: I don't get it, Herb. What do you mean?

Herb: I get the impression that something else is at stake here, Craig, not just your relationship with Mika. I get the impression you are testing. She always has to be there when you want her, she has to be with you on your terms, down when you're down, not enjoy herself unless you do . . .

Kate: What would you fail, Craig, if you failed?

Craig: I'd think I just wasn't good enough for her. It would add one more time to the times I haven't measured up. You know Herb, I'm always afraid I'm not going to measure up.

Herb: I know that, Craig. I feel what you're saying. I really do.

Kate: What about Mika's part in all this? I don't think we ought to focus the whole conversation in on Craig, as if it is all Craig's doing. Whatever Craig is doing, Mika can't seem to handle it. I admit it's not easy. I'm sure you're as confused and upset as Craig is.

Mika: I just feel so much pressure, and when I'm beginning to have a good time I think of him and wonder if he's all right, and then I stop myself from having a good time anymore.

Herb: Okay, but you are stopping you, not Craig. Whatever his thing is, it isn't stopping you, and I think Craig ought to know that.

Craig: Okay, I see that. That's logical.

Herb: Logic doesn't always touch what's happening inside you, Craig.

Mika: You can't always explain how you're feeling. I can't anyway. Especially when I'm feeling shitty or he's feeling shitty. And when we're feeling OK we just don't think about it anymore.

Herb: Well, what would you like to see happen, Mika?

Mika: Just that I could be able to have fun when I want. If I want to be with someone else—it doesn't matter if it's a girl or a boy—I don't want to have to worry about Craig getting upset.

Kate: But that's your thing, Mika, not his.

[Mika turns to look at Kate for the first time.]

"I know, I know, Mika, but look, Craig isn't stopping you from being with someone else. He doesn't like it, but he can't really stop you and I think he knows it. I think he knows you get upset when he's down so all he has to do is be down. Sort of play down, really.

Craig: That's not fair, Kate. I don't do it deliberately. You make me out to be a real bastard.

Kate: I know you don't do it deliberately, Craig. I know that, but it always seems to happen, doesn't it? Well, then, maybe you make it happen without really knowing it.

Craig: You mean because I know she'll get upset?

Kate: Maybe. You know, both of you, hard as it is I think you've got to talk things out with each other, try to tell each other how you feel, how *you* feel without putting the other person down.

Mika: I'd just like to have fun with Craig. I don't want it to get deep or involved. That's not what I want right now. I don't think I could handle all that psychological stuff anyway, I get confused by it.

Kate: Do you get confused by my asking you not to put Craig down for how he feels?

Mika: Oh no, I understand that. You can't say so-and-so doesn't have a *right* to feel what he feels. That would be stupid. If he feels it, it exists, it's true for him anyway. At least that's the way it seems to me.

Craig: Does everyone go through this kind of stuff?

Mika: I think it's partly because we're young.

Kate: I agree. It's a hell of a job for someone your age.

Mika: Do you and Herb go through this kind of stuff, too?

Herb: If you want something with each other, at whatever level, young or old, there it is and it isn't always easy by any means. Sure we go through it. People are pretty much alike in this. I'll try not to be complicated. People who want to share things or have a life together go through pretty much the same sort of things. How you feel about each other, how you think the other one feels about you, how you sometimes get in each other's way and all the rest is part of . . . well, discovery.

Craig: Well, there's a lot to think about. I think I've sort of had it for now, for this evening I mean.

Mika: Yes, I think I'd like to stop now, too.

Craig: Why don't we just go on back down the hill now.

Mika: I guess Craig and I just want to be together now.

ENTRY III

Two private lessons this morning. Marti in math, Bob also. Followed, after lunch, by a private talk with a twelve-year-old boy who thinks he wants to leave at the end of the term. He has only been here a year, and he says the school has nothing more to offer him. I do not believe that this is true or that it is his true reason for wanting to leave. I deliberate whether or not to tell him what I think his real reason is.

This is always a touchy matter. For one thing, I may be wrong. For another, even if I am right, how much good will it do to tell him, how much can he accept of what I feel about him? As long as the intuition is mine and not his, he would be right to reject it. There is something beginning to happen in George, just beginning, and this is precisely what I think he does not want to face and why I think he wants to leave.

George is not a dull-witted boy or a stubborn one or even a particularly angry one. He is alert, good-looking and likable. The trouble is he has to be on top of things all the time, and that is not easy to accomplish here at Lewis-Wadhams because no one notices whether you're on top of things or not. No one cares about it or values you because of it. George came here, bringing with him his "leadership qualities" (I quote from the record of his previous school, a Midwestern junior high in an affluent Lake Shore suburb).

Had his educators forgotten their own childhood? If you have leadership qualities at twelve and you know it, how do you go about dumping them? How do you goof off if you want to? How do you quit having to excel? How else can you measure yourself? How can you begin to do something simply because you like doing it? Besides, who are you supposed to lead? And where?

I told George simply that I hoped he would decide to stay. We like him. I like him. He knows this. He said he really likes it here too. He really does—he said—but he just doesn't know.

Someone passed by the window and hollered in to "Come on down to the soccer field, Georgie."

"I'll talk to you again, Herb."

"Any time, George."

I think George's self-image is slipping. I think it worries him. I think he is beginning to enjoy himself.

Item: The dilemma youth is caught up in today. They must take themselves enormously seriously (by whose standards?) and contemplate from the age of twelve on, if not younger, endless vistas of excellence. The cloistered halls are it, for year after year after year. I am not putting down mass education. "Higher" education, that is. I am saying that the relentless push for it today conceals a wish—or a need—on the part of our technological society to prolong adolescence, a postponement of maturity which serves (whose?) interests.

I have a certain nostalgia for the thirties. It was not all bad then. Children working by the time they are sixteen or seventeen is not necessarily a terrible thing, terrible only if the need to do so comes out of hunger, privation, discriminatory practices. Out of that kind of urgency, yes, it is terrible. But there are other, inner urgencies today's postponed adulthood does not meet. I am not at all sure many children do not need to make adult extensions by the time they are sixteen, do not need to participate on a nonchild level, to take themselves seriously and to be taken seriously for who they are and what they want, to accept responsibility for their choices, in education, in work, in sexual involvement.

There are no choices for youth today. There is, at eighteen, only the alternative of books or guns.

Item: Very much on my mind this last week is the episode of "Guns in the Hands of Blacks" at Cornell University. What a furor. Because of the presence of guns? If so, it is worth considering that the enormous outrage expressed against this symbolically violent act of an admittedly oppressed minority contrasts oddly with the outrage expressed by most of the same people (a percentage of upstate New Yorkers) *against restriction* of the right to bear firearms. Everywhere one went up here last summer and on into fall before the elections, one came across posters plastered on upright surfaces from garage doors to board fences to drugstore windows: "If guns are outlawed, only outlaws will have guns!"

Guns were not outlawed. This is hunting country, it is said. I do not like to see guns in the hands of blacks or whites. Guns produce their own kind of hate and fear. We have enough of both in these United States today. The culture breeds hate, and we all live with it, in one form or another. Perhaps dramatic confrontation is inevitable from time to time, perhaps even necessary. I think America has its tolerances—political, economic and moral. Those who cry out that what is happening on college campuses is neo-Nazism do us all a disservice. This sort of accusation is a great fear-breeder. Hysteria breeds hysteria. We do not need it.

Sadder to me than anything else about this fracas was the

statement, "Cornell has only three hours to live!" To assume that there *is* life in a system which negates dignity and individuality, due process and liberty, is theatre of the absurd.

Item: A related absurdity is the persistent rumor that A. S. Neill is dead and Summerhill is closed. I get one or two letters a week telling me this, and over the last six years have answered literally hundreds of questions put to me by people I meet at educational conferences or lectures or informal meetings with parents and educators, mostly from the latter. Would they prefer Neill to be dead and Summerhill to be canceled out? One is finally forced to come to this reluctant conclusion, for no vigorous denial on my part, and presumably on the part of others including Neill himself, has been able to put paid to the story.

"I've heard people say I am old and senile," Neill said recently, "which I am not. But if I were, it doesn't negate what Summerhill has done all these years."

One cannot wish it away, the alive and vital force of the free school movement. One cannot wish Neill and Summerhill away. They have to be dealt with, the life-style of the free school, its educational philosophy measured against that of the Establishment School. It is no use saying "don't rock the boat." The boat has already been rocked.

I think we may one day look back on this period of our history as one more example of man's desire to affirm life without really knowing how. A black studies program isn't going to do it, neither is the mea culpa reaction of the guilt-stricken white man. What is, then? Nothing, if not the release on an unconscious level of the hate and violence that symbolically enslaves us, the restatement on an unconscious level of the wish to live.

Thursday, 1 May—
Sunday, 18 May

ENTRY IV

Thursday, May 1st, 9:00 P.M. A fitting day to talk about revolution.

Kenneth Keniston writes about student unrest:

> All revolutions draw upon older values and visions. Revolutions do not occur because new ideas suddenly develop, but because a new generaton begins to take old ideas seriously. . . .

A new generation taking old ideas seriously inevitably begins to question the failure of the older generation. "They failed" translates on a personal level to "They failed *me*."

We talked at tonight's discussion about personal blame. Who is to blame? "My parents." "Society." The twin monsters young people blame for, among other things, their own failure to experience satisfying and sustaining relationships. I take the view that in time young people will have to deal directly with society and with their parents. In time, they will be able to effect changes and they, in turn, will be held responsible for what they achieve or fail to achieve. This is on the revolution-making level. I do not think it (necessarily) solves personal frustrations. You have to come to terms with your own feelings of guilt, or of shame on a personal level, no matter who is to blame. The feelings are yours, not your parents', not society's.

The image of a flawed parent is hard for a child to face.

He is hurt by it. He discovers his parents make mistakes and are not always nice people. Certainly not gods. The hurt child is angry. His own feelings become damaged. He absorbs a double guilt: theirs, and his for seeing theirs.

Alone, he does not feel strong enough in himself to deal with this. Most of the time he's going to repress what he feels, push it down out of sight. He is only one of him—weaker, younger, defenseless, frightened. Alone and a child, he maintains his silence and his hurt.

Collectively, he feels stronger. Collectively, youth is beginning to demand basic changes, to strike out against hypocrisy, dishonesty, corruption—moral as well as political. I think much of the energy expended by young people against their parents and society is a misdirected effort to solve personal frustrations. The "generation gap" is not so much a gap of years as of emotional separateness. Look at the anger, bitterness, contempt, and perhaps saddest of all, indifference that goes pouring into this gap.

I do not want to imply that student unrest is solely triggered by emotional frustration, or that the blindness of the older generation to the young is not hugely responsible. I do think a young person who is helped to face his personal dissatisfaction on a personal level and to confront his personal feelings of anger and guilt on a personal level will be freer and more effective in his revolutionary struggle for social change.

Who is to blame becomes almost irrelevant. But then, the need to blame is a compound of many things.

Entry V

You can walk through the main house on a warm and lovely Sunday like today and meet scarcely anyone. Someone may be at the piano in the lounge—Louise, perhaps, and Beethoven, Chloe beating out rock, or, as today, Annemarie making up her own airs and singing to herself. There will be someone in the kitchen getting Sunday night supper. Often, as this afternoon, it is Jane, largely silent, dreamy, smiling vaguely at me as I pass on through to the cooler. There are beginning to be more and more speckled brown eggs piled in open cartons on the shelves now as the new hens begin to acclimate themselves to the "free run" they have of the hen yard.

The Sunday silence of the main house says—if nothing else about Lewis-Wadhams does—that it is spring term. Outdoors, the woods and trees are beginning to breathe again. Everything is softness and pale greens, sunlit, earth-smelling, humming. The air full of flutter and gentle commotion and the distant sounds of children's voices.

The weekend visitors have gone. Visitors come with warm weather, and by and large are welcomed. Particularly if they have been invited. Note the literal interpretation given to the "freeness" of a free school, taken to mean anyone can drop in who happens by. A spring oddity—the number of people who happen to be in the neighborhood or just passing by Lewis-Wadhams over a warm and sunny weekend. Yet we are located a good five hours' drive from New York, three hundred miles from Boston, even thirty-five miles from neighboring Vermont.

Curiosity about us, most of it honest and informed, some of it merely prurient or plainly hostile, is so widespread that if we had no rules regarding visitors, we would be flooded by same. A surprising lot of people who say they have respect for children's rights—to privacy, for example—and honestly think they mean it, behave on premises as if they were observers admitted to an avant-garde zoo. Children are quite patient with this sort of thing. I am less so. Between us—staff, administration and children—we've come up with a fairly workable set of visitor regulations. They represent so large a majority of community feelings as to be considered a consensus.

They are: Visitors allowed only on weekends. Anyone wanting to sleep in school must have permission from community. No meals served to visitors unless paid for and there is enough food prepared so that no member of Lewis-Wadhams is shortchanged. Visitors only allowed during the week with permission of community. No visitors allowed in classes without permission of the specific class.

I used to worry about Lewis-Wadhams being considered an unfriendly place to visit. I don't anymore. Unfriendly people bring their unfriendliness with them. This weekend two young men from an upstate teachers' college expected around two o'clock Saturday afternoon arrived at my front door early Saturday morning before we were altogether out of bed. With Sigrid in my arms clamoring for breakfast, Duggy yapping and three hungry cats surging around my ankles, I suggested the visitors might be a little early, and would they please come back later.

Undisguised hostility: "Isn't there another school around here where we won't be asked to leave? We'll visit that one."

"Do so. And if you can't be more courteous, don't bother to come back."

The subject of hitching rides came up at a Saturday meeting a week or two ago. Children, and once in a while staff, like to hitch rides to Elizabethtown with visitors. A few pros and cons, then the resolution passed: You can ride with visitors who have insurance and who can be trusted.

A perceptive ruling on counts emotional as well as practical.

We have letters of thanks from visitors and we have letters

beginning, "I'm sure you don't give a damn what visitors think of your school, but since it's a free world there's something I have to get off my chest. . . ." Happily, the numbers of those disappointed by the way a free school looks, acts and feels— and angered by their own response to us—are more than compensated for by those who value "the friendliness and warmness, the openness and honesty, polite but untarnished by false civility . . . a thing of love and happiness. . . ."

A strange and unhappy incident took place last year, the only time the community has ever called a special meeting at which it was voted to ask visitors to leave. The experience was hurtful all around.

Two young men had come for the weekend, one a recent graduate who wanted to go into teaching and begin his teaching life at a free school. I think, looking back on the episode, that both of them were overwhelmed by the openness and candor of the place, by the physical freedom, by their own desire to become part of what was happening—to be liked and accepted.

What happened in reality terms was perhaps nothing. In fantasy, or in emotional terms, it was devastating. One of the two young visitors, caught up in his enthusiasm for what he felt all around him, "Like," he said, as nearly as I can remember, "an outpouring of life and honesty and love, feelings of love, wanting to be close, touching one another," had yielded to his own spontaneous impulse to put his arms around a teen-age girl and caress her. She was, very simply, frightened.

The young man accepted the truth of this—she *was* frightened. What he did not understand was why the community chose to support her in the face of his denial that he had "meant anything by it"—anything harmful, that is. Confused and hurt, he could not accept the verdict without wanting to defend himself against it and asked to be allowed to do so at a second meeting. The verdict was unchanged.

Later, before they left, we talked about it. We talked on for a good hour or more. He wanted desperately to understand. Why had they not been able to accept him? He had been open with them, open about his desire to be accepted, to be part of them, to express his own feelings of love and tenderness, open about his own hurt that he had been misunderstood.

To be open, to be young, to be free, is also to be vulnerable. In the end, that was really about all I could say.

ENTRY VI

Spring fever when I was a kid was called indolence or plain laziness, by teachers and parents and elderly relatives who seemed to get particularly petulant and restive when the warm weather came.

In school one got bawled out for nothing things like daydreaming, half falling asleep in study hall most of the time. This was called inattentiveness and was a punishable offense. People did it anyway. There was not much else to do (where I grew up) about spring fever. A notable absence in my neighborhood of fields to run through, streams to fish in, ponds to wade across, other half-naked kids to splash water at, frogs to throw rocks at, minnows to scoop up and so on. Those kids who had bicycles nine times out of ten had a paper route to work or after-school deliveries to make for the grocer and butcher shops. Grass in anyone's backyard meant getting out the lawn mower. Hammocks, if there were any, were for Father or Uncle and their like.

I am sympathetic to middle-aged city-bred people like myself who still suffer from spring fever. We'll never catch up.

The rhythm changes in Lewis-Wadhams come May, and so do the concerns. A culling from the Minutes of Saturday's meetings:

26 April
Barb: Concerned about number of pets underfoot since beginning spring term. Seems all congregate in kitchen. Seems that way.
PROPOSAL: They all leave.
PROPOSAL: They all stay. CARRIED. RIDER: Keep out of Barb's way.

3 May
Ezra: Wants hammock
PROPOSAL: We buy one out of games money. CARRIED.
Herb, Dawn and Jim on pets.
PROPOSAL: No more pets at all. Sybil cannot replace her cat. CARRIED.
PROPOSAL: Bob's cat can be replaced. CARRIED. DIED.
PROPOSAL: Eve's cat can be replaced. DEFEATED. Uncared for!
RIDER TO PROPOSAL #1: Animals for class, chickens, ducks, sheep, etc., are okay.

10 May
Berube: 2/3 community rule for vote not working for Saturday meeting. Not enough people come.
PROPOSAL: Drop rule for spring term.
PROPOSAL: Rule stays same as always. CARRIED.
Eve: On swimming alone.
PROPOSAL: None.
Jed: On dropping the shoes off-property rule.
PROPOSAL: We can go off-property without shoes.
PROPOSAL: Drop subject.
No vote.
Ezra: On hammock. When will games committee buy one?

17 May

Herb: On bicycles and parts. People are swiping same.

PROPOSAL: We put name tags on bicycles, ditto parts. CARRIED.

PROPOSAL: We have welding class. CARRIED.

Brin: On Saturday meetings.

PROPOSAL: You can carry on Saturday meeting with anyone who shows and you can vote.

PROPOSAL: No change in meeting rules.

PROPOSAL: On Saturday you need at least 22 people to vote. CARRIED. RIDER: Weekday meetings keep old rule.

Bob: On hitching outside 30-mile limit on weekends off.

Herb: You can hitch if you want to, but that's between you and your parents.

Pete: On camping out rules.

PROPOSAL: People can camp off-property with parent permission overnight. RIDER: Be back by 9:00 next morning. CARRIED.

RIDER: Camping not allowed in vicinity of diner, etc. CARRIED.

RIDER: Camping not allowed in vicinity of houses of staff, neighbors, etc. DEFEATED.

Ezra. On hammock.

PROPOSAL: Donna and Jed, games chairmen, work it out.

PROPOSAL: Ezra takes $6 from games fund and buys one. CARRIED.

Pets, off-property rules, swimming rules, bicycle rules, keeping supper for people who stay out late fishing, bicycling, walking, etc., continue to be discussed at special weekday meetings. Regular business last week or so includes for me seemingly endless conferences with staff and students engaged in seminar workshops to take place next four to six weeks. Most of them off-premises. Logistics of transportation a problem as ever. Foresee urgent need for (a) small school bus,

(b) new pickup truck, (c) second station wagon, (d) more staff with own wheels and driving licenses.

St. Regis Reservation: A two-day camping trip planned by Paul Berube with Dome kids. First days: Onchiota, New York, three-hour drive from Lewis-Wadhams. Visit Indian Museum. Camp out. Second day: Early start for Reservation. All-day visit with Mohawk Indians. Welcome extended to Lewis-Wadhams group. Six signed up. Paul's long stay on Cheyenne Reservation and many, many reminiscences of Indian ways and sensibilities well known to everyone here. A chance for our children to participate in Indian life with someone on the inside. I wonder, though, if Paul is still bitter —disappointed—that the Cheyennes never granted him total acceptance. Do they, or would they, any white man? What is Paul expecting from the Mohawks? Hope not too much.

Adirondack Project: A three-week workshop fór eleven- to fourteen-year-olds. Bunny Ring has worked up bibliography, schedule of places in Adirondack region to visit and people to talk with. Permission being sought from parents to allow children to fly in private plane during last week in seminar to be able to take in a few out-of-the-way places. Region is rich in historical sites, also museums showing how people lived, loomed cloth, cooked, etc. The eighteenth century is very much alive up here in traditions, landmarks, families. Tentative dates for seminar: 15 May through 1 June. Talk of children making up newspaper as record of experiences. Will look into printing press possibilities. Old one here, may still work, ask Clyde and Dave. *The Adirondack Gazette,* they are calling it. Twelve kids are signed up.

Overnight Hike: Hartman taking a group, teen-age, on overnight hike up Mt. Marcy. Dates depend to some extent on weather. Probably mid-June.

Survival Week: Dave Reuther and I will go to Montreal with twelve members of Survival Seminar: Marti, Craig, Jake, Mimi, Jason, Fleur, Red, Eve, Brin, Sam, Tim, Tina. At the first meeting of the group at the end of last term, survival in a city was talked about, which has more relevance to today and to this particular group (all city bred) than living on berries and leaves and roots in a return to nature. Common fears were exposed. Again makes one question the depth of sophistication of apparently cool-cat teen-agers. The innocence and unsureness of the adolescent. Mostly fear of people, it turned out, with these youngsters.

It was decided that it was time to face hang-ups instead of sitting around rapping and saying to each other, Yeah, I'm afraid too. So what do you do about it? Answer: Try to survive in a strange city, a foreign one like Montreal, for a week. Go about singly or in pairs during the day. Evenings, meet for dinner, discussion, compare experiences and lend one another a little moral support for the next day.

Volunteers took on assignments for finding out about transportation possibilities and expenses, border regulations, rooming houses, culling newspapers, travel guides, maps, French-English phrase book, etc. Brin will write a letter to the mayor about our proposed visit. Eve made a list: "What Kids Are Afraid of in the City," and people checked it off. Here it is:

	Afraid	*Not Afraid*
+ + + + + + + +	Meeting people	Directions
	Drunks	Hitchhiking
	Being jumped	Police
	Being gypped—restaurants	Shopping
+ + +	Police	Walking around
	Trains/buses	
+ + +	Shopping	
	Germs	
+	Toilets	
	Hoods	
	Black people	
+	French (vs. American)	
	Sophistication of Montreal	
+	Rape	
	Getting lost	
+	Directions	
+ +	Dirty looks	
	Getting stalked	

Sex and Sexuality: The last meeting of the year. A smaller class than usual, we met by consensus this evening, after dinner. A farewell, in a sense, as several of the older ones— Craig, Annemarie, Sam—won't be back next year. Craig will probably go on to art school, Annemarie and Sam still in doubt.

It was easy talk, and not very much of it. More a being together. Eve had written something she wanted to read and get people's feelings about. Sex versus love—or, perhaps, love versus sex. Are they inextricable?

> When someone says "I love you," and plays at being close to you when all they want is sex, then that is *using* and that is cold-hearted.
> But if you understand they want to kiss you just because

you turn them on, how can you be used? You can only be used when there is a form of a lie. . . .

We talked about what made a person feel like an object and why. We talked about the feelings of loneliness or indifference which came about as the aftermath of a relationship devoid of tenderness and compassion. About sex in the absence of friendship.

Some children talk freely, almost boastfully, of their experiences. How much is fantasy? How much is hearsay? Hard to say. Contemporary mythology deifies the cool ones.

Annemarie said, "If you peel back the supercool, you find anger, and when you peel back the anger, you find a scared little kid."

(To take at face value a child's bravura can be to deprive him of the support he is asking you for. This support may be no more than to know that you, the adult, are strong enough, secure enough, and have good enough feelings about yourself to be able to love him. Without falseness.)

Monday, 19 May—
Friday, 30 May

Entry VII

A soft and beautiful quiet spring rain has been falling on and off for most of this fifth week of the year's last term. Gentle rains seem to go with things ending. Not quite so around here. It has been, again, a week of many happenings.

There follows a sparse account of same, before I succumb, as have Sigrid, Kate and our assorted animals, to the seductive and sleepy sounds the rain is making against our high arched roof.

Item: Jason has gone at last. There have been so many meetings called against him since spring term started that all seem to blur into one great fiasco. A little kid in tears. Jason bullying again. A school meeting assembled. The vote unanimous to dismiss him.

Jason: "Oh, well, one more school. So what?"

Jason's parents: "We just paid you the last installment on his tuition. Do we get it back?"

Item: A first time. Chloe and Harry, blue jeans, hair hanging down back, barefoot, fishing in the Bouquet River. Arrives a carload of high-school boys from a nearby town, five sixteen- to seventeen-year-olds. They are drunk, and what followed was the sad cliché scene of loud and insulting sex talk, threats, obscenities. Chloe is thirteen. So is Harry, who looks ten, and they must have thought him a girl too. Wisely, he did not disabuse them of this notion.

I heard about it only after they had talked to a few of the older children down the hill and had been urged to come to me with it.

Free school equals free sex is a myth we have long ago lived down amongst our neighbors. Neighbors, by the way, include the State Police as well as other local officials. I had no hesitation bringing charges for harassment against the boys involved.

The judge heard us in his chambers. Chloe and Harry told what had happened. There was no shame.

The boys shuffled about from one foot to another and said they were sorry. A couple of beers was the trouble. They were paroled in the custody of their parents. No one was angry. It was over in half an hour. The judge asked how the fishing was, and we went home.

Item: Breaking and entering. Again a brush with the law. From the other side, this time.

Different Lewis-Wadhamites have different favorite spots to fish in. Some like the cascades and deep pools where the water runs fast in the narrow channel over rocks and between the tall pines under the wooden bridge. Others like it a mile or so further downstream where the Bouquet widens out and loafs along through the meadows down by the Northway. The attractions of the latter are several. It's an easy bike ride from school—no steep grades. You can loll around in the grass if you don't feel like fishing or the fish aren't biting, and if that bores you too, finally you can peer between the cracks of the boarded and shuttered windows of the big white frame house on the knoll above the river. Typically, this would and did interest two little hoods like Donald and Steve. With hero-worshipping eight-year-old Pete along, they went further than the usual furtive inspection and speculation as to who lived there, if anyone, in summer, what was inside, whether it was ever occupied, or if it was haunted. Resting their bikes for support against the *No Trespassing* sign, they decided to bust in. It was not an easy task. An iron bar had to be forced, a window climbed through and the front door opened from the inside. The next obvious step—to make off with enough loot to prove oneself a crook in good standing.

So far this is reconstruction on my part, from what was told to me later. The loot, a pitiful assortment of battered pots and pans, a couple of thin, gray summer blankets, cutlery and useless odds and ends, was subsequently passed around the main house for inspection, then stashed away. Ultimately I was called to the scene.

The collection was thereupon reassembled. The three boys and I loaded it into the car and went back to the summer house, where we replaced the stolen goods, put the iron bar back into place and returned to school.

To find six-foot State Trooper John Farraday waiting in the kitchen. The boys had been seen. There were forms to fill in, a report to be made out, and back we all went once more to show John what had been taken and where it had been replaced. The charge was a serious one, and the forms went off to the judge of the Family Court in Ticonderoga. Breaking and entering was no joke.

The verdict of the school meeting called on Don, Steve and Pete was succinct and simple. People said:

"Assholes. If you have to involve yourself in that kind of thing, if you have to be a crook, keep it on school grounds."

PROPOSAL: The three be fined to stay on school grounds for two weeks. CARRIED.

Reflections on stealing: There is a rash of it this term. Meeting after meeting has been called and generally a pragmatic view taken, i.e., give it back, pay for it, be fined for it, work it out privately, form a search committee, get a strong box, and face the consequences!

There is on-property theft and off-property theft.

There is little kids' thievery, sometimes called "borrowing," only the property somehow doesn't get given back to its original owner.

There is thievery for fun, thievery to outwit rules and locks and staff people.

There is thievery to get attention.

There is thievery because it is easier to take than to ask for.

There is thievery from thieves.

There is thievery which is imaginary. This is victim-hero thievery.

There is thievery which is revenge. This is the "rip-off" against society.

There is ideological thievery. This is "what's yours is mine" and, uncommonly, "what's mine is yours." (When it involves off-property thievery, can be considered a variant of the "rip-off.")

There is gang thievery. This is by ten-year-olds, generally outgrown by age eleven or twelve.

Although treated somewhat lightly here, thievery is never treated lightly by the victim and we, as a community, do our best, although not always successfully, in having the stolen property returned and the thief apprehended.

ENTRY VIII

Tuesday. The deadline for defection from Survival Week, agreed on by all, passed without casualties a week ago. Yet Jake and Marti announced yesterday they had changed their minds.

"The trip won't do anything for me," Marti said and shrugged it off.

"I don't need it," said Jake. "I know how to get around a city. I live in one."

Neither of these statements came across to me as anything but cop-outs. At a meeting called for last night I said just this.

We are set to go in little more than a week. All the logistics have been worked out and the arrangements laid on. They are:

Everyone is to go by train except for David and Herb. We

are to drive up, bringing food for snacks and breakfasts.

Everyone is to take $40.

Cost of lodging per person is $3 per day.

We are to stay in a rooming house recommended by the Chamber of Commerce. It is ten blocks from the main drag, two blocks from the Metro, thus accessible to all of Montreal, including Expo and McGill University. McGill has figured in most of our preexpedition talks as a likely source place for meeting people and finding out where the action is.

Three rooms have been booked, one for David and Herb, one for the boys, one for the girls. The boys' room—the largest—has an icebox in it.

The meeting turned me down flat right at the start. I had no right to object to Jake's and Marti's withdrawal.

Mimi: It's none of your damn business, Herb. They've a right not to go.

Tim: Shit, man. Lay off.

Eve: If they want to cop out, like, that's their right.

Brin: We're not uptight about it, why are you?

Herb: I grant them their right not to go, but I'd like to know why they've decided not to. I think I have a right to question their decision. Suddenly they just don't feel like going. Is it purely arbitrary? I don't think it is, and I don't think it adds up that suddenly the trip has ceased to have meaning for them.

Eve: Isn't that their business, Herb? They're entitled to their privacy. You can't make them go.

Craig: I don't think that's Herb's point, Eve. I don't think Herb wants to make them go.

Sam: No one wants to make them go.

Mimi: Do you, Herb?

Herb: No, I don't. I don't want to make anyone go. I

simply would like them to tell me—to tell us—why they've changed their minds.

Jake: Okay, you bastard. Why do you think we don't want to go?

Herb: I'll give you my thoughts as long as you're at least willing to listen without feeling put down!

Marti: Fair enough, Herb. I'm willing to listen.

Herb: I think you're scared. I think you're both scared and I think you're scared to confront your fears. I think you're running to cover. I don't believe your cool. I don't think you're really indifferent or as sophisticated as you make out you are. I think you're as uptight as everyone else is about how you'll make out on your own in Montreal. Only you won't trust yourselves enough to let your fears out. You don't trust the rest of us to support you. You don't trust the caring . . .

Marti: All right, Herb, I guess it's your privilege to feel any way you want to about me, but it's mine to do as I choose.

[Pause. Shrug.]

I just choose not to go. That's all.

Everyone appears suddenly to have nothing more to say. A long silence. It is broken by:

Mimi: Okay, let's let it go then!

Jake: I don't want to hassle it anymore. I'll go.

Mimi: Do you want to?

Jake: I said I'd go, didn't I?

Mimi: That's not what I asked you. I'm asking you if you want to go.

Jake: If I want to go now? Okay, Mimi, I want to go.

Sure, I want to go now. Does that make you feel better?
Herb: Come on, man, does it make *you* feel better?

Jake's reply was lost as the meeting broke with others talking and laughing. Marti remains unflappable. I think of what Annemarie said about peeling back the supercool and finding a scared little kid. Marti is not coming back next year. Perhaps she is right to hang on to her cool a little while longer.

Late afternoon. The sun breaks through dissipating clouds and the whole place begins to shimmer. Branches and the eaves drip. The new grass is polished to a high gloss. Duggy dashes frantically in and out of the dog door. The cats creep out. Sigrid splashes about in the puddles the rain has left behind along the driveway.

Along about five-thirty, Mac and Steve appear at the back door with a week's catch of rainbow trout. A weary Hartman is already wrapped around his second can of beer, feet propped up on the deck rail, watching the sun go down. Kate willing, we have company for dinner. The trout disappear in swift and concentrated silence.

The day and the week end with the appearance of Donald and his sleeping bag. He has been fined to sleep up the hill with us for the last few nights. His bedtimes have been rough on everyone in the main house. Here he seems to sleep peacefully.

Kate and I have been talking of initiating a cottage program as soon as we can afford to put up a couple of new domes. The littlest ones and possibly the restless ones might have a better chance of survival here. Donald is not coming back next year and I have my doubts about Steve.

ENTRY IX

Friday to Sunday. A beautiful and capricious spring weekend. Friday and Saturday the sun full out, Sunday a steady downpour. Hartman and seven youngsters were drenched by the time they got home from a three-day bike trip to Vermont. Ditto those trout fishing along the Ausable River with Dave Reuther.

Monday. In the mail this morning came a letter from the Israeli Government Tourist Office. They will be glad to assist us in finding a kibbutz. Our plan for next winter has been accepted. For details I am to write to Mr. Zvi Dagen, Director of the Youth and Student Department. The kibbutz welcoming committee will be ready to meet our group at the airport. There will be no cost for room and board if our students will work six hours a day.

Mika is ecstatic. So is Berube. So, as a matter of fact, am I. (Exuberant, anyway. A little old for ecstasy, I say to myself. It is not true, though. I think I would just like to be going too.)

ENTRY X

Donald and Steve have decided to leave before the end of the term. I had not the heart to ask them to stick it out. Since the breaking and entering episode, they have not been able to settle down at all, trout fishing notwithstanding. Have we failed them? They say doctors bury their failures, architects display theirs, what about schoolmasters? It is always a hard thing to face.

ENTRY XI

Pandemonium, righteous indignation and hoots of laughter greeted the discovery today (Friday) that Don and Steve have made off with the strongbox containing some $75 worth of allowance money. A note in the place of the strongbox said simply "Up Yours," signed "Donald and Steve." An instant decision was taken through a school meeting to alert the Albany police, have them board the train the boys were on and recoup the money. This was done. Two plainclothesmen found the boys, held the train, and called me to find out what we wanted done with them. The fact that we had no intention of prosecuting the boys but simply wanted the money back seemed "highly irregular" to the law. We got about $60 back. They had spent the rest and thrown the strongbox out the window.

I would be happy to report that the story ended right there. But it did not. Steve's father wanted a tuition refund. Tragically, he asked no questions about his son. No "How come," "Why," "What happened." Just a demand for a return of his fees. He didn't get it.

Sunday, 1 June—
End of Term

ENTRY XII

A beautiful Sunday in the North Country. The spring rains seem to have gone for good, leaving the skies washed clear, the sun full out day after day. It is warm now and smells of summer. A headline in today's *New York Times*: "Students to Gain a Voice in U.S. Education Policy," followed by an interview with the new U.S. Commissioner of Education, James Allen. Allen was a good man as Commissioner of Education for the State of New York, on balance generally supportive of the child and of the nonconforming teacher. I hope he lasts in Washington. Few do who refuse to close the doors on new ideas, who remain responsive to people, students, in this case.

Bruno Bettelheim in *Children of the Dream*:

> The child who receives ample dependent intimacy from his parents . . . can one day begin to spend it on his peers, who can give little in return. This deficit in peer life has to be replenished by the parents, until such time as the other peers, their emotional storehouse overstocked too, can give in return. And when the peer can freely give to the peer, both are fully grownup.

All of our experience at Lewis-Wadhams bears out the truth of Bettelheim's statement. Those children who have the roughest time here, who are the least able to give and at the same time the least able to receive (an even sadder handicap in my view), are those who have suffered emotional abandonment in early childhood.

Bettelheim goes on to speak of equality:

> It is the experience of having been given to for years in a dependent intimacy that permits us, in adulthood, to trust in mature intimacy. We can give freely because we are sure we will eventually be given to, in return. But a child who has lived a life of equality receives no vast surplus of what I have called here dependent intimacy, and without it he cannot later afford to give it to others.

I take issue with his statement that children in a kibbutz are reared in "equality." Equality and egalitarianism are not synonymous. Equality in childhood does not mean sameness, nor does it mean a bargain between parents and children vis-à-vis the amount of giving and getting, nor does it mean the equality of expectation. It means that children are people, and as people their feelings and desires, wants and wishes, are quite as valid as those of the adults who are their parents. Once you accept this emotional parity as the essence of what is meant by equality, you are then able as a parent or parent-substitute to begin the hard work necessary to give the child fully and freely what *he* needs without needing to receive quid pro quo.

The right to life, liberty and the pursuit of happiness implies, in individual as well as social terms, diversity rather than sameness. Sameness is conformity, not equality. Equality is recognizing that every human being, from infancy to old age, is equal to every other human being in his emotional right to search out what he needs—to nourish his life-force, to fulfill himself. Therefore, to my mind, if children were reared with equality as I define it, they would be fulfilled in their infant needs.

Entry XIII

Montreal, Tuesday morning. Everyone met for supper last night. We had picked a Hungarian restaurant known to have good, cheap food and a warm, homelike atmosphere, red-and-white-checked tablecloths, friendly waitresses, huge helpings and an infinite number of courses. There was music, and to everyone's amazement wine and beer were served with no questions asked as to anyone's age.

Later, as planned, we all went back to the rooming house to talk. Most people had started off alone in the morning, then by prearrangement met up with someone else for the afternoon. The self-assigned tasks included taking the Metro, talking with a stranger, going into a place which presented a sort of challenge of the unknown, exploring French neighborhoods. As though to make things even harder for themselves, or perhaps to provide themselves with an automatic alibi in case of failure, the group had decided against learning any French. They wanted, they said, to see if they could get along without it.

Jake was the first to set off yesterday morning, by himself, as much as to tell all of us that, OK, he had agreed to go even though he did not need the experience and now he was going to show us his cool was real.

This morning Brin was odd man out. He stayed in bed later than everyone else, and left the rooming house by himself only a few minutes ago. Very gutsy. He has no map, and no real inner direction at the moment. Yet off he went down the street as though he'd lived here all his life. I watch him as he gets to the corner. He hesitates, then heads for the Metro.

Tonight we meet at a Chinese restaurant, then come back here for more talking.

Here are some of the things people said and talked about at last night's meeting. Some talked from notes they had made, others did not. Almost everybody's self-assigned project for this first day out included going about Montreal on foot, by subway and bus, eating lunch out somewhere—and meeting people. The general scheme—the morning to be spent alone and the afternoon with somebody else—did not always work out that way. By choice? By accident? It is hard to say.

Eve and Tina

Eve: Well, we went to McGill University. We walked all around. Like Washington has Dupont Circle and Boston has Harvard Square, but Montreal doesn't have any place like that.

Sam: Did you go to the Student Union?

Tina: No. We just walked down this street and we saw this guy in the window and he was leaning half out of the window. He was writing something.

Eve: He looked just, like, really neat because he was writing and we were going to go up to him and ask what he was writing and we couldn't. We were trying to convince ourselves: OK, what if we make a fool of ourselves, we could always run away. We decided not to, that we couldn't right then, and we made a promise. The next person we see that either of us want to go up to, we have to.

Herb: Then what happened?

Eve: We looked down the street and we saw a couple. Right, Tina?

Tina: Uh huh, that's right.

Eve: They were walking down the street. They were getting closer and closer. And we were getting tighter and tighter. Finally they crossed the street and we burst out laughing. We sat down on the sidewalk all relieved. Then, later on, we went back up the street and we did talk to that guy.

Craig: How did you get to talk to him?

Tina: We just walked up to him and asked him what he was writing. He started to ask us questions and we asked him questions and he invited us inside his apartment and asked us if we wanted some tea.

Eve: We were there for about an hour. He was, like, young, twenty-four or something. He was teaching. He taught high school and he didn't like it. He just needed the money. He was really neat and then his girl friend came in and she was nice too.

Most of the thing is that I would never have gone up to him if I wasn't with Tina.

Tina: The same with me. I wouldn't have gone up to him if I wasn't with Eve.

Craig: Is it because you're a girl that you're scared?

Eve: It depends. That's not most of it because the people I usually want to go up to don't look lecherous or anything.

Tina: Those types are the ones you *don't* want to meet.

Craig: What about this guy?

Eve: He seemed like he would be easy to go up to but we were just too scared.

Tina: The people you really want to meet, they don't seem to care. I'm really glad we did like we planned to, Eve and me. I feel really good about it.

Mimi

Mimi: Well, I started out and everyone was gone so I was alone and I was exhausted. I was so tired and I was very depressed walking along that absurd street and it was practically raining. I was walking down the street—you know, the rich streets—and I went to the bathroom in the Metro. All morning I had a really weird time.

Eve: When you were all depressed in the morning, Mimi, was that because you wanted to be with someone?

Mimi: No, it was because I thought it was the most absurd thing in the world that I should be in Montreal and in a rich neighborhood and the rain. I was so depressed I was just sort of like numb.

Herb: Scared?

Mimi: Scared of what?

Herb: I don't know. I'm asking you.

Mimi: Lots of things scared me, so I went on the train and I went from Frontenac to Atwater. That was my project for today, to explore a neighborhood. The only thing I liked about it was the spiral staircases. I just kept going back and forth on the Metro. Then I wished I had somebody to joke with about how absurd it was.

Brin: I don't see why you thought it was so absurd.

Mimi: I just think that the city is very absurd.

Brin: You mean the idea of cities?

Herb: What stops you from going up to somebody, Mimi?

Mimi: I didn't see anybody. Well, you know, like it's one of my big problems.

Herb: May I suggest that you go with somebody else tomorrow?

Mimi: What's that going to do?

Tina: It helps a lot, Mimi. I didn't think it would, but it does.

Mimi: I know what it's like to be with somebody but I just wish I could go by myself and do the same things, but I can't.

Tina: If you can't, then the second best thing is to go with somebody else and start just being with them, and then you just get to be yourself after a while, after you feel more comfortable about being around people. I couldn't have done the things that I did today if I was by myself. At least I did those things and I really feel good that I did them.

Mimi: But I really wouldn't want to go with someone else. I'd want to go by myself.

Dave: Did you eat by yourself?
Mimi: No, I didn't eat.

Craig

Craig: I didn't meet a lot of people. I only met a couple. Then when it got to be time to start coming down this way on the bus again, I got really, really down like before, but I thought, Oh, God, never mind, soon everyone is going to be looking human again.

Then a woman sitting across from me sighed and she reminded me of someone I know and we looked at each other and smiled. She was old and she was knitting and she was human-looking.

That's the thing I noticed most and I wrote about and I couldn't understand. People's faces look like they bow to their feelings. I'm not sure if it's in me or if it's real.

One more thing. Everything that was happening to me all day really helped me to write. At first I was just writing details and then I got to writing stories. At first I was writing what I was doing and then my feelings really came out.

Jake

Jake: I didn't want to write. I just didn't want to see on paper again what I had been doing. I just didn't want to think about it.

I remember one thing that summed up my whole day and my feelings about Montreal, and I still have that feeling. I feel detached from everything going on and I try to mix and it was just strange I couldn't mix at all.

I was getting tired of observing everything, just walking around doing things and looking at people and looking for places to go, and not being part of it. It's like when I take pictures, I'm not involved with it, I'm detached from it. I went up to a whole mess of people, like ten people all day, and I· just tried to talk to them. I don't really know how I started, I just walked up to them. Half the people just walked away. I started talking and they just left, and the other people moved around on the chair or looked at me like I was crazy or something. It was really a drag. I just didn't want to talk anymore.

I've been trying to think why I got so upset with it and the reason is I think because I don't know if I had a kind of screwed-up attitude to begin with. I *felt* all right when I went up to people to begin with. I didn't *think* I was being too aggressive or approaching them in an obnoxious way, but they got totally put off anyway.

Brin

Brin: Two main things I'm afraid of are being rejected, and failing. I'm afraid of this trip, that I'll just go to stores and say "that's nice." I say to myself nothing can happen and I try to do things. I think I'm just as scared as I was.

Mimi: First I want to know what is success and what is failing?

Brin: Failing would be going on this trip and not doing anything or meeting anyone. Success would be going on this trip and meeting people and making friends.

Mimi: I want to know what you're scared of.

Brin: I'm scared of failing. I'm scared of being rejected.

Mimi: What happens to you when you get rejected?

Brin: Nothing. Sometimes nothing. Sometimes I really feel bad. Like if I go into a store or something . . .

Mimi: No, listen, this is a different kind of question. The question is, when you get rejected what happens *inside of you?* What changes take place in you? How about fantasy? The fantasy where you're really, really rejected by somebody?

Brin: Okay, I can tell you what would happen. I'd be afraid to do the same thing or something like it. That's all.

Mimi: No. I mean, how do you feel right then, right then when you're being rejected?

Brin: Well, there are two different things that bother me in going up to a person and trying to talk to them. I feel bad if I'm rejected then. I don't know if it has something to do with a personal thing, a personal sort of thing about me, and that's why I'm rejected. Or it isn't really me they're dealing with but, like, my actions, the way I act or what I say and not who I really am.

Mimi: Talk about the personal thing because I think . . .

Brin: I'd feel pretty bad because I'd think that either they weren't seeing me as I am or they weren't seeing me as I think I am, and I would feel bad about it either way, because I'd still doubt me.

Mimi: How would you doubt yourself?

Brin: I would think maybe I was a shit. Since they think I am shit, maybe I really am.

Mimi: Oh, so when someone rejects you it's just your own self-pity.

Brin: It's my self-doubt, not self-pity.

Mimi: I don't think you've said what you're scared of yet.

Brin: You mean specific things?

Jake: He did. Lots.

Mimi: He did, but it doesn't seem very tangible.

Eve: It isn't very tangible. Like, I'm afraid that if it works out here when I'm with someone else, when I get home and

I'm really trying it at home or something, I'll just find out that it's just a farce.

I don't know, that's the whole thing. Whether it's really working or not because here I'm with someone and at home I'm not with someone. Because at home there's nobody with me and I'm lost, and here when there was nobody with me I was lost too.

Mimi: People think little lost, fatherless, motherless, all alone, lost in the great big city. Like, no mother is going to come and no father is going to come. Maybe you're going to need somebody like that but that is not really going to fill it in for you. So you have to learn how to fill up this thing for yourself. You have to be your own mother and your own father when you need it. Which is something that is missing in you that makes you feel these things.

Herb: I want to comment on something. Some of you seem to agree with the conclusion that something is missing and because something is missing you are then fucked-up.

There does not necessarily have to be something missing. There are very real fears and there are those fears which seem to have no basis in reality.

If a truck is coming down the road and you're standing in the middle of the road, you have a real fear that you can get killed. Now that's quite real and the fear is not generated because something is missing.

With Brin, his fear is symptomatic of something else. I'm not sure whether we can or should talk here and now about the total feelings of rejection Brin has. He doesn't know why they are the way they are or where they come from.

Brin: I can guess.

Mimi: If he can guess, he can know.

Herb: It's up to you, Brin. If you want to, go ahead.

Brin: It might be, like if I go by the idea you're not a whole person until you're old, then all this stuff in your early childhood might be it.

Herb: All this stuff?

Brin: Like early rejection.

Herb: Do you feel that?

Brin: I don't know. There are other things besides that.

Herb: What are they?

Brin: Mother and father and the things that influence you when you're young. I don't know what they are because I don't remember. Things like that. Rejection when you're young by influential forces. Then you'd be afraid to try again.

Herb: This is you, Brin? Something you're thinking, not something you've read about somewhere?

Brin: Some of it I've read. I think I've thought about it. I still don't know.

Dave: By influential forces you mean teachers, parents, things like that?

Brin: Yeah, and I sort of hope it's not my parents. I don't think it is, but it could be. It might be and that's the thing that scares me. I'm not sure exactly how my parents felt when I was born. I know how they are now. I'm pretty sure about that.

Like I said before, one of my big fears is that right now I trust my parents and love them a lot, but I'm afraid they might have messed me up when I was little, and also in school people would say, you love your parents. Oh God, I guess that sort of ties in with it.

There are a lot of images people have about parents and I've been exposed to a lot of them, and sometimes you get the general idea that your parents are no good. You absorb some of that feeling.

Mimi: Do you feel bad for your parents that they rejected you?

Brin: I feel bad because I like my parents and I don't want them to mess me up.

Mimi: What do you mean? It's like "I love my parents but I hate them." It is because when people reject you, you get mad at them and you don't want to get mad at them?

Brin: Yes. I don't want to hate them.

A lot of talk then from almost everybody about parents, about childhood, about the things that were expected of one, about the relevancy or irrelevancy of one's early feelings to one's experiences in Montreal. About adolescence. About growing up.

ENTRY XIV

Back at Lewis-Wadhams. Another beautiful Sunday. Almost the last one of the term. Cloudiness. Quiet. Hot. Almost everyone is out fishing or swimming.

From my office I can hear Annemarie at the piano in the Little Room. She will be graduating, leaving here for good, in another two weeks. She is playing and singing one of the countless tunes she has composed in the course of her three years here. Like many of her tunes, this one seems to have a sadness to it. Is the sadness in her or is it in me? Do I hear it that way today because the year is almost done?

One year, really only eight months, from September to June, one year out of six. It's been full and fulfilling.

The only reason for living is being fully alive;
and you can't be fully alive if you are crushed by secret
   fear,
and bullied with the threat: Get money, or eat dirt!—
and forced to do a thousand mean things meaner than your
   nature,
and forced to clutch on to possessions in the hope they'll
   make you feel safe
and forced to watch everyone that comes near you, lest
   they've come to do you down.

Without a bit of common trust in one another, we can't
   live.
In the end we go insane.
It is the penalty of fear and meanness, being meaner than our
   natures are.

To be alive you've got to feel a generous flow,
and under a competitive system that is impossible, really.
The world is waiting for a great new movement of gener-
   osity,
or for a great wave of death.
We must change the system, and make living free to all
   men,
or we must see men die, and then die ourselves.

D. H. Lawrence
1929